"If there is anything the contemporary church has proven, it's that you cannot create a leader in a classroom. Dr. Klopp takes the discussion of leadership out onto the playing field. As one who has been coached by his ministry playbook, I can tell you his strategies put points on God's game board."

Dr. S. Craig Bishop, senior pastor,
Branch Creek Community Church, Pennsylvania

"Henry Klopp pours wisdom, refined through focused research and years of effective church consulting, into this valuable book. He tackles tough church leadership questions, rips away superficial, easy answers, and offers challenging, practical direction for pastors who are serious about leading. Dr. Klopp reviews and applies current leadership theory with a solidly biblical understanding of church leadership. *The Leadership Playbook* should be read and applied by any church leader motivated to serve with greater effectiveness."

Jared Roth, vice president and chief operating officer,
International Church of the Foursquare Gospel, Los Angeles

"Henry Klopp, the consummate coach, has provided a biblical road map for team building. This book will provide invaluable insights for any church leader who wants to build an effective ministry team."

Stan Toler, author and pastor, Oklahoma City

"Leadership! We talk a lot about it but seem to do very little. *The Leadership Playbook* may turn that all around. Not only will it help you define Christian leadership, but you'll also learn the transferable principles that can be used to build leaders in any church context—large, medium, or small. *The Leadership Playbook* is a vibrant new resource that you must put on your reading list this year. Better yet, put it on your list this month!"

Gary L. McIntosh, author and professor,
Talbot School of Theology, La Mirada, California

"*The Leadership Playbook* is not just another book on leadership. Combined with his rich experience as a pastor, consultant, and coach, Henry Klopp has done the hard work of researching the most compelling literature and leadership models available today. Excellent reading for leaders and emerging leaders in the twenty-first century!"

Dr. Gary B. Reinecke, coauthor
of *Developing Coaching Excellence*

"Finally, a book that is not another popularization of ideas lifted from the latest business texts. This book can be your own mentor-coach to equip you to be the best pastor-leader possible. Henry Klopp esteems pastors as God's gifts, and he loves Christ's church so much that he is passionate that she be blessed with excellent leadership. I, for one, am the better for his efforts."

Mark Slomka, pastor,
Mount Soledad Presbyterian Church, La Jolla, California

"Some authors write from their experience alone, others from their predictions. Dr. Henry Klopp is one of few able to write with hindsight, insight, and foresight. I have known Dr. Klopp since his first pastoral assignment. To me he has been a pastor, trainer, advisor, and friend. The words he writes are more than knowledge; they are passionate discourse to the hearts of leaders, for whom he cares deeply."

Joe Woodruff, president,
Next! Innovations, Inc., Puyallup, Washington

THE
LEADERSHIP
PLAYBOOK

THE
LEADERSHIP
PLAYBOOK

A GAME PLAN FOR BECOMING
AN EFFECTIVE CHRISTIAN LEADER

HENRY KLOPP

BakerBooks

Grand Rapids, Michigan

Published by Baker Books
a division of Baker Publishing Group
P.O. Box 6287, Grand Rapids, MI 49516-6287
www.bakerbooks.com

Printed in the United States of America

Library of Congress Cataloging-in-Publication Data
Klopp, Henry.
    The leadership playbook : a game plan for becoming an effective Christian leader
/ Henry Klopp.
        p.   cm.
    Includes bibliographical references.
    ISBN 0-8010-9157-8 (pbk.)
    1. Christian leadership. I. Title.
BV652.1.K595 2004
253—dc22   2004014344

CONTENTS

INTRODUCTION

- **LESSONS FROM MY COACHING BACKGROUND**
- **PERSONAL PARADIGMS**
- **SUMMARY**

There are many people who can talk about leadership, theorize about leadership, and debate over leadership, but very few people are doing and living leadership.[1]

Tony Evans

He who thinketh he leadeth and hath no one following him is only taking a walk.[2]

John Maxwell

The leadership crisis of our times is without precedent.[3]

Robert K. Greenleaf

Tom was the founding pastor of a very successful church ministering primarily to people in their twenties and thirties. In less than three years the church had grown to more than four hundred people. The church had developed a very unique vision for ministry that was able to reach a significant number of unchurched people. Yet in the third year Tom resigned to go into a secular vocation.[4]

Ralph was the long-term pastor of a large evangelical church in the suburbs of a large city. The church had an unusual number of key lay leaders, including several who were involved in leadership positions in the church's denominational headquarters. The church was wrestling with the decision to expand its facilities, and two individuals had offered one million dollars each for the new facility. However, that facility was never built because of ongoing conflicts in the church primarily centered around one very influential family. After many years of struggle Ralph decided to try ministering in a different church.

♟ ♞ ♟

Sam was the founding pastor of an incredibly successful charismatic church. The church had grown in twelve years to more than five thousand people and was well known not only in its own denomination but also to other churches around the country. However, behind the scenes were serious levels of conflict regarding the leadership style of the pastor. Key staff and lay leaders wanted to see a different style of leadership and pursued this agenda over several years. Eventually the senior pastor left the church as the conflict became more and more public.

♟ ♞ ♟

Ben was the pastor of a large mainline church that ministered in a very wealthy suburb of a large metropolitan area. The church had a significant history and was well known throughout the area. The church was also well known within its denomination, as it was a leader in trying to move the denomination toward a more conservative heritage. However, in the church itself, despite several efforts, they could not coalesce around a clear vision for its future. A major attempt at fund-raising for future facility needs was quite unsuccessful. Multiple agendas operated within the staff and key lay leaders, which continually stalled any significant progress.

♟ ♞ ♟

Mike became the new senior pastor of a church that had seen several pastors come and go over the years. Mike was recognized as one of the brightest young men in his denomination. He had excelled academically and was a very gifted communicator. When Mike was interviewed, the church leadership indicated that they wanted an aggressive pastor who would lead them into the future. After two years of total frustration and very little accomplishment, Mike left the church and took the senior pastor position in another church.

These churches have at least four things in common.

1. They are all churches I have worked with in a consulting capacity. (names changed for obvious reasons)
2. They all suffered from internal conflict or lack of direction or both.
3. They all were pastored by devoted servants of God whose personal lives and the lives of their families were testimonies of total Christian commitment.
4. They all had senior pastors and key leaders who wrestled with issues regarding Christian leadership.

Probably no issue raises more debate and diversity of opinion than that of Christian leadership. It's no wonder pastors and ministry leaders are confused and struggle so desperately in this area. The result is a conspicuous lack of genuine leadership in the church, however. This lack of leadership is not limited to the church. Many writers have identified a leadership vacuum in our society. Most of our organizations and churches are overmanaged and underled. And because so many pastors and ministry leaders believe leadership is nothing more than power and control, they mistakenly fail to provide the necessary leadership.

As a consultant I have worked with churches of all types and sizes and in a variety of geographical locations. I never cease to be surprised by the confusion I encounter regarding Christian leadership. The fact is that in spite of all the literature on leadership in both church and secular circles, pastors and ministry leaders remain confused about what leadership means for them. The following is a list of common concerns expressed by ministry leaders:

- How should the unique characteristics of individuals (their demographic profiles, socioeconomic backgrounds, educational credentials, experiences, beliefs, etc.) affect their leadership roles and styles?
- What is meant by "leadership style"?

- What is the connection, if any, between "personality style" and "leadership style"?
- Is leadership a "learned" or "innate" behavior?
- How does the gift of leadership fit in with leadership roles and functions in the church?
- Why are parachurch ministries attracting some of our best leaders who used to be serving in churches?
- Are there common characteristics of effective leaders, particularly effective Christian leaders? If so, what are they?
- What is the difference between leadership and management?
- We hear the term "servant leadership," which is commonly applied to leadership roles in the church. But what are the practical day-to-day implications of this term?
- The Bible uses the concept of the leader as a shepherd. What are the implications and principles that this model of leadership supports?

While many more questions could be listed, it is obvious even from this short list that there is a great deal of confusion and frustration regarding leadership issues in the church.

Plenty of books are available on the subject, even in church circles. In fact, an incredible number of such books are available. The problem is that these books often contradict each other. If we were to go to a Christian bookstore, we would find three types of books written on ministry leadership:

1. Books that study particular biblical leaders and attempt to discern the leadership principles that can be learned or inferred from their lives.
2. Books that focus on leadership issues or problems in the church and then define solutions that implicitly or explicitly define "correct" leadership behavior.
3. Books written by Christian leaders, often pastors of large "successful" churches, who share their personal backgrounds and experiences and define how they approach ministry. Assumptions regarding leadership style and behavior are usually not discussed directly but sometimes can be inferred from what is written.

Those who have done extensive reading in any one of these categories can attest to the confusion that can ensue. What one book recommends, another book condemns. What one book lists as key principles are totally ignored in another.

An additional problem for Christian leaders is what to do with all of the writing and research from secular sources regarding leadership. Basically, most Christian leaders choose one of three paths.

1. **Rejection of all material that is not Christian.** This protects Christian leaders from being unduly influenced by secular sources. At the same time, however, there is a real danger of legalism and isolationism that prevents these leaders from taking advantage of all the resources that are available.

2. **Immersion into the secular world.** The advantage here is that Christian leaders now have full access to all sources. At the same time, however, there is a real danger that they will be influenced to adopt principles and practices that are not in alignment with Scripture.

3. **Critical evaluation.** This is a middle ground that must be defined by Christian leaders. It takes advantage of all sources but at the same time critically assesses the principles and practices based on scriptural truths.

This book uses the last of these approaches, recognizing that not everyone will agree with this choice. However, keep in mind the following scriptural principles.

- Avoiding evil does not mean we have to withdraw totally from the world. Jesus Christ and Paul are living examples of people walking this middle ground. Christ avoided all evil but not all sinners; to do this was interpreted by many of the religious people as evil. Paul also resisted the attempts of false religious leaders to keep him from interacting with the secular world.

- As Christians we are free to disagree and challenge one another's thinking within certain limits (cf. Luke 7:33–35; Acts 24:16; Romans 14; and 1 Cor. 9:19–23).

- Interacting with the world is not the same thing as identifying with it.

- We must never sacrifice truth to gain approval.

- We are not to judge our brothers in debatable areas; we must let God do the judging.
- We should never violate our own conscience in the area of doubtful things, but we should be willing to challenge our "comfort zone."

To ignore all of the research and writing that is available from secular sources would be foolish, but, as you will see, to accept all of it without critically judging the content would be just as wrong.

Lessons from My Coaching Background

One of the things I have seen in ministry settings over and over again is the applicability of principles I learned and used as a Little League and high school coach. I have coached at every age level from age nine to senior high and have coached three different sports (football, basketball, and track). Even when I was a pastor and church consultant, I helped coach football at a local high school.

It always amazed me how close athletes get to their coaches. Years later, many of these athletes still come up and reminisce about the good old days. I saw the effect a coach can have on the lives of his players. When I became a pastor and consultant, I often pondered what I learned from the coaching profession and what, if anything, was applicable in my work with churches. My conclusion is that the model of coaching is very transferable and a model to which we can refer as we try to discern how to be leaders in our churches today.

Personal Paradigms

Although we would all like to believe that we are objective, most people realize that their background experiences color the way they see things. When my wife and I came to Christ in our midthirties, with virtually no spiritual background, our world was literally turned upside down. We immersed ourselves totally in the church world. In fact, in just over a year I was asked to join the staff of a large church as pastor of evangelism. I realize that as a result of my personal background and spiritual heritage, my paradigm of the church has certain distinct features:

- I view the church as an agent of change in its community. I see the role of the church not just to exist but to make a significant difference in its ministry area. I don't see the church as a fortress, protecting itself from the world, but as a force going forth to transform its world. Sunday is important, but the real battles occur Monday through Saturday.

- I view the church as adaptable, flexible, and able to contextualize its ministry in every cultural setting. I am excited about the many different models of ministry I see and feel no compulsion to get back to the good old days or try to define a single biblical or New Testament model for church life. I view change as a positive and energizing facet of church life.

- I do not believe the primary purpose of the church, or at least the institution of the church, is to meet people's needs. The church will never be able to meet all the needs of its constituents. Instead, I see the church as a place where people are challenged and equipped to meet their own needs and the needs of others. I believe it is the responsibility of every Christian, not just the paid staff, to pray, serve, give, evangelize, disciple, study, worship, counsel, and comfort others. Christians who are not doing these things on a regular basis are unhealthy spiritually and need to be aware of such.

- I believe that churches should be the best examples of leadership in every community. After all, we have the Word to teach us how to lead, and we have the Holy Spirit's guidance every minute of every day. It's a shame that pastors and ministry leaders have to look to the secular world for models of effective leadership. It should be the other way around. People in secular fields ought to be looking at ministry leaders to find out how to lead effectively. We have all the necessary spiritual resources that should allow us to be incredible leaders. Leadership in our churches should be exemplary in every way. The fact that it isn't is a sad commentary on where we really are.

- While conflict is a natural part of human life and interaction, the church should be a living example of how to manage conflict. Christian leaders should understand conflict and be able to lead effectively in the midst of most conflicts.

All of these beliefs seem reasonable to me. It did not take me long in the consulting field, however, to discover that few churches I worked with operated from the same perspective as the one represented by the above list. I recognize, therefore, that as you read this book, your own set of presuppositions and beliefs will influence the degree to which you can relate to the concepts I present.

Summary

This book seeks to address the key issues and concerns pastors and ministry leaders have regarding Christian leadership behavior. In the process of learning about these issues and concerns, readers will learn how they can become better leaders. The following are the major objectives of this book:

- To define the confusion that exists in the area of Christian leadership and answer the question, why?
- To discuss the leadership vacuum in our churches today and understand why it exists.
- To understand ministry leadership structure and organization from a biblical perspective with a particular emphasis on understanding the church of the first century.
- To bring clarity to the issue of Christian leadership and define principles that are both transferable and replicable.
- To examine what concepts and principles are transferable from the field of coaching to ministry leadership.
- To examine how God trains Christian leaders.
- To understand how to implement proper leadership principles in the life of the church.
- To understand the major obstacles and hindrances that derail many Christian leaders.

Questions for Reflection

1. Think about the major questions you have regarding Christian leadership. What are the ones that frustrate you the most?
2. Why do you believe there is so much confusion in the church regarding Christian leadership?
3. What are your personal paradigms regarding leadership and particularly Christian leadership?

1

LEADERSHIP ISSUES IN OUR CHURCHES TODAY

- ■ LEADERSHIP BEHAVIOR OR STYLE
- ■ LEADERSHIP BEHAVIOR OR STYLE IN MINISTRY
- ■ BEHAVIORAL STYLE
- ■ BEHAVIORAL STYLE IN MINISTRY
- ■ SUMMARY

I am convinced that believers will not experience the joy and satisfaction of authentic ministry until they are serving Christ in ministries consistent with how God designed them: with their spiritual gifts, passions, temperaments, talents, abilities, and leadership styles.[1]

Aubrey Malphurs

If you take the high road, you're bound for authentic living. That's a road where you're able to look at your past honestly, learn from it, grieve over parts of it if needed, but then move on in a healthy way.[2]

John Trent

Leadership is initiating—going out ahead to show the way.[3]

Robert Greenleaf

As you approach your fourth decade, you begin to think a lot about who you are and where you are going. It is inevitable, and I believe, universal. Some people approach this period in life pathologically and call it a crisis. I regard it more positively and call it halftime—an interval in a person's life where he or she explores ways to transform their success into significance.[4]

Bob Buford

Doug was the pastor of an incredibly successful church. It had grown to be one of the top two churches in its denomination. Doug was very easygoing, and the church had developed a vision for ministry that focused on a healing environment. People flocked to the church to become part of this warm, inviting, and nurturing climate. Doug's leadership style tended to mirror both his personality and the church culture. However, the church reached a point where it faced a very difficult issue regarding relocation and building a much larger facility. Like many pastors, Doug was somewhat overwhelmed by the thought of such a large project but saw no other alternative. As the project began to develop, it became larger and larger and was obviously going to require significant financial resources. Doug felt subconsciously that his normal leadership style would not provide the necessary momentum for such a large project, so he tried to adjust it to accomplish the new task. He began to speak and lead much more aggressively. Unfortunately, in a very short period of time, the church was in a state of confusion, and Doug suffered a heart attack that almost ended his career.

The best place to start in order to understand the problems and issues regarding church leadership is to take a realistic look at what is happening in our churches today. Research done by the Barna Research Group found that:

- Less than one out of every ten senior pastors could articulate what he believes is God's vision for the church he is leading.
- Only 5 percent of senior pastors say they have the gift of leadership. Most pastors thought they were neither called to nor divinely equipped for that post.
- The typical pastor works long hours (more than sixty hours per week) but devotes less than ten hours per week to leadership activities.[5]

Todd Hunter, a leader in the Vineyard Church movement, studied church planters who had failed. His research showed that:

- Ninety-five percent of these pastors were unable to identify, recruit, train, and deploy workers and leaders.
- Seventy-seven percent of these pastors had no clear plan and goals, which resulted in working hard at wrong things or lack of focus.
- Sixty-eight percent of these pastors were using a nurturer/enabler/facilitator style rather than a more assertive leader/equipper style.[6]

From these and other sources, it is not difficult to conclude that most pastors serving churches today are not really leading, although they hold a position that requires vital leadership. While much less research is available regarding nonpastoral leadership in the church, it appears that the problem is equally severe in this area as well.

In my work as a church consultant and from personal observation and empirical research, I am convinced that pastors and ministry leaders are genuinely confused about what Christian leadership means and what they should or should not be doing.

- First, many pastors and ministry leaders are using leadership styles that are not going to work in most settings.
- Second, many pastors and ministry leaders are operating from personality styles that are not truly their own.
- Third, many pastors and ministry leaders operating from genuine personality styles are trying to lead with leadership styles that are destined for failure.

The combination of these elements produces Christian leaders who are ineffective and frustrated, while those who follow them are genuinely confused.

Leadership Behavior or Style

In the secular marketplace the terms "leadership behavior" and "leadership style" have become part of the common vocabulary. Both terms refer to how leaders lead. While models and descriptions of leadership behavior or style abound, the most popular model today is one based on research done at Ohio State University in the 1960s. It has become well known because of the writings of Ken Blanchard, Paul Hersey, and others.

This model has become extremely popular in the business world, but interestingly it has also become very well known and accepted in Bible colleges and seminaries. For that reason, we need to understand the concepts behind the model as well as its implications.[7] The diagram below helps explain the model.[8]

(High)		
Providing Supportive Behavior (Relationship Behavior)	High Relationship and Low Task (Supporting Style)	High Task and High Relationship (Coaching Style)
	Low Relationship and Low Task (Delegating Style)	High Task and Low Relationship (Directing Style)
(Low)		

(Low)   (Task Behavior)   (High)
Providing Directive Behavior

This grid is based on two dimensions: directive behavior and supportive behavior. The authors define these two dimensions as follows:

- *Directive Behavior*—The extent to which the leader engages in one-way communication; spells out the role of the follower(s) and tells the follower(s) what to do, where to do it, when to do it, and how to do it; and then closely supervises performance.
- *Supportive Behavior*—The extent to which the leader engages in two-way communication, listens, provides support and encouragement, facilitates interaction, and involves the follower(s) in decision making.

In addition to the styles mentioned in the diagram—directing, coaching, supporting, and delegating—the authors of this model have introduced a fifth leadership style that is foundational to their theory of leadership. It is called *adaptive* or *situational* leadership and is based on the development level (or what some term the *task relevant maturity*) of the follower(s). Development level refers to the ability, understanding, and skill of the follower(s) on a specific task and can vary from task to task. In the opinion of the authors of this model, effective leaders are constantly assessing the development level of those they are leading. They then adapt or adjust their leadership style according to this assessment. The four development levels, from low to high, and the authors' recommended leadership style for each are as follows:

- *Low Competence/High Commitment*—The group being led has minimal understanding and ability with the task at hand, however, they are interested and highly enthusiastic as they approach this task. The recommended leadership style would be the Directing Style.
- *Low to Some Competence/Low Commitment*—The group being led has some understanding and ability with the task at hand, however, they have little interest and enthusiasm as they approach this task. The recommended leadership style would be the Coaching Style.
- *Moderate to High Competence/Variable Commitment*—The group being led has moderate to significant understanding and ability with the task at hand, however, their interest and enthusiasm varies as they approach this task. The recommended leadership style would be the Supporting Style.
- *High Competence/High Commitment*—The group has significant understanding and ability with the task at hand and is highly interested and enthused as they approach this task. The recommended leadership style would be the Delegating Style.[9]

The underlying concept of the situational or adaptive leadership model is that the leader must change or adapt his or her behavior based on the development level of the follower(s), with a focus on providing an environment that encourages the follower to move from the low development level to the high development level. In other words, first the leader must determine the development level of the group he or she is working with, then use the appropriate leadership style, while at the same time elevating the development level of the group so they require less and less directive behavior from the leader.

As mentioned previously, this leadership theory is well known both inside and outside church circles. In fact, it has become the primary leadership theory taught in our Bible colleges and seminaries to prepare those who are moving into church ministry.

Unfortunately, this theory *has never been proven to work in any setting.* In the authors' own research manual, one of the researchers acknowledges that this leadership model has only been measured against the *perception* or *satisfaction* of the *followers*, not on any objective or subjective measurement of the actual *output* of those followers. In other words, the followers felt better about their leaders, but we don't know if the followers accomplished any more. One of the researchers said, "In the business world, bottom line output measures sometimes appear to be stronger evidence than do the subordinate's perceptions of satisfaction."[10] If the research had focused on areas that directly affected people's ability to do their jobs well—not just how "satisfied" they were—the results might have been substantially different.

Unfortunately, this leadership model, to which most pastors have been introduced in their training, does not have the necessary research to support its adoption and use in either secular or church settings. Still, the leadership behaviors in this model deserve closer attention.

Leadership Behavior or Style in Ministry

Books and articles on ministry leadership tend to cluster around the five leadership behaviors identified in the previous instrument. The problem, however, is that each of the five behaviors or styles has its own supporters who claim theirs is the best or most biblical model. My own empirical research indicates that while the adaptive/situational leadership style is the primary one taught in Bible colleges and seminaries and seems to resonate well with most pastors and ministry leaders, it is *not* the predominant style being used in ministry settings.

The following is a description of each of the leadership styles with some specific application to leadership in the church environment. I also will include quotes from authors who seem to favor each style.

Directing Leadership Style (High Directive and Low Supportive Behavior)—CEO Model of Pastoral Leadership

1. The pastor or church leader provides specific instructions and closely supervises task accomplishment.
2. This style focuses on the pastor's or leader's role as initiator or director.
3. A typical sequence would start by the leader saying, "I've determined we have a problem. . . . Here is what I think we should do. . . . Any questions?" The leader would then facilitate discussion, trying to make sure everyone on the team understands and agrees with the course already determined by the leader.

Robert Schuller seems to reflect this style of leadership when he says, "Leadership is the key to church growth, and what is leadership? Leadership is thinking ahead, planning for the future, exhausting all possibilities, envisioning problems and dreaming up solutions to them, and then communicating the possibilities and the problem-solving ideas to the decision makers. This is leadership. In any institution, the leader is the man who is thinking ahead of everyone else."[11]

Coaching Leadership Style (High Supportive and High Directive Behavior)—Coaching Model of Pastoral Leadership

1. The pastor or church leader initiates action but looks for significant input from others.
2. This style focuses on the pastor's or leader's role as coach, leader, or equipper.
3. A typical sequence would start by the leader saying, "We've determined we have a problem. . . . Here is what I think we should do. . . . What do you think we ought to do?" The leader would then facilitate

discussion, trying to get the team to arrive at a decision that is mutually agreeable.

"In America," C. Peter Wagner states in one of his many books, "the primary catalytic factor for growth in the local church is the pastor. Vital sign number one of a healthy, growing church is a pastor who is a possibility thinker and whose dynamic leadership has been used to catalyze the entire church into action for growth."[12]

C. B. Hogue also seems to argue for this leadership style when he states, "Pastor and congregation should walk in a horizontal relationship. But the effective, evangelistic pastor will walk in front. His practices will reflect his beliefs, his emphases will mirror his ideals. He will be the catalyst, through study and prayer, opening his church to the indomitable dream of church growth, his will be the equipping, the empowering role."[13]

Supporting Leadership Style (High Supportive and Low Directive Behavior)—Chaplain Model of Pastoral Leadership

1. The pastor or church leader helps and supports the group's efforts toward task accomplishment and shares responsibility for making a decision with them.
2. This style focuses on the pastor's or leader's role as servant-leader, facilitator, or enabler.
3. A typical sequence would start with the leader saying, "We've determined we have a problem. . . . What do you think we ought to do?" The leader would then facilitate discussion, trying to get the team to arrive at a consensus. The leader may or may not share his own opinion, and if he does, he'll wait until everyone else has shared first.

Larry Richards appears to support this leadership style when he writes, "Jesus sets forth a relationship between leader and people in which servant-leadership is to prevail. The leader in this case is not over but among people. The role is not of authority but of service. . . . Such a leader is a facilitator—enabler—equipper; his role is that of helping the body of people become functional in achieving their purposes."[14]

"The servant-leader," writes Joe Ellis, "helps the body of people perceive their goals, develops commitment to them, mobilizes to reach them, and pursues their achievement. He offers guidance, inspiration, instruction, and resources; but he strives to work in cooperation with the group as a team."[15]

Delegating Leadership Style (Low Directive and Low Supportive Behavior)—Congregational Model of Pastoral Leadership

1. The pastor or church leader turns over responsibility for decision making and problem solving to the group.
2. This style focuses on the pastor's or leader's role as threat reducing or noninvolvement.
3. A typical sequence would start with the leader saying, "We've determined we have a problem. . . . You need to decide what needs to be done. . . . Any questions?" The leader may or may not facilitate discussion and would seldom if ever share her own opinion but holds the team responsible for coming up with a decision upon which they can all agree.

"I believe," writes Larry Richards, "that the pastor should view his role in the church moving toward renewal, as that of a change agent. As a person who seeks to involve the congregation in a self-motivated and self-directed change effort, and to reduce the tensions which change will cause . . ."[16]

Adaptive/Situational Leadership Style (Variable Supportive and Directive Behavior)—Management Model of Pastoral Leadership

1. The pastor or church leader adapts his leadership style according to the development level or task relevant maturity of his group or team. Thus, the leader could use any of the preceding four styles after determining the development level of the group.
2. This style focuses on the pastor's or leader's role as analyzer/adaptor.

As previously mentioned, Paul Hersey and Ken Blanchard are strongly supportive of this leadership style. The following is their rationale: "An effective leader is able to adapt his style of leadership behavior to the needs of the situation and the followers. Since they are constants, the use of an appropriate style of leader behavior is a challenge to the effective leader. The concept of adaptive leadership behavior might be stated as follows: The more a manager adapts his style of leadership behavior to meet the particular situation and the needs of his followers, the more effective he will tend to be in reaching personal and organizational goals."[17]

Ted Engstrom also seems supportive of this style when he writes, "During periods of rapid growth and expansion, autocratic leadership may work very well. For example, the founder of a new Christian organization or the founding pastor of a church is often a figure with charisma, who knows intuitively what is to be done and how to do it. Since the vision is his, he is best able to impart it to others without discussion. But during periods of slow growth or consolidation, the organization needs to be much more reflective to become more efficient; participative leadership may be in order. Since organizations have difficulty continually changing their leaders, it follows that those leaders will need different styles at different times. The appropriate style depends a great deal on the task of the organization, the phase of life of the organization, and the needs of the moment."[18]

Lastly, Jack Balswick and Walter Wright seem to support a similar view: "Although a key dimension of pastoral care is leadership, because of the complexity of congregational life and diversity of individual parishioner needs, effective ministry often demands a variety of leadership styles. . . . It is in this collective sense, when all four styles of the leadership continuum are exercised in a congregation, that ministerial leadership is directly related to the potential development of Christian maturity in congregations. . . . A church which is being led with only one style of leadership cannot increase the spiritual and leadership maturity of its members."[19]

In my own empirical research and work with churches, I discovered an amazing phenomenon. When measuring the leadership behavior using the instrument previously described, pastors and ministry leaders are almost exclusively using one leadership style (supporting). The coaching and adaptive styles are used somewhat but not even close to the frequency the supporting style is used. This is not true when we look at the research done in nonchurch settings. The interesting question is why?

Some have tried to explain the difference by saying that in business you are dealing with paid employees, while in ministry you are working almost totally with volunteers, which makes the organizations quite different and therefore requires different styles of leadership behavior. While I have not done extensive research in the area, I do not believe this is the answer, because my work with leaders in parachurch ministries indicates a much different profile.

I think the primary reason pastors and ministry leaders use the supporting leadership style is because the typical church culture believes that this is closest to the "servant-leader" or "shepherd" model that is normally taught as the biblical model. Pastors and ministry leaders learn quickly when they begin to lead that the more directive styles are contrary to the popular culture and organizational design of the typical church. Thus, there is an amazing similarity in the leadership behavior or styles of pastors across the board, regardless of size, denomination, or geographical location. Of course there are notable exceptions, but the pervasiveness of this one model is quite incredible.

Now the really bad news. In the empirical research that I have done, the *least* effective leadership style in churches is the one being used the most—the supporting style. This held true regardless of what criteria was used to measure effectiveness.

There's an obvious flaw when a leader relies solely on the affiliative [supportive] approach: Work takes second place to feelings. Leaders who overuse this style neglect to offer corrective feedback on performance that could help employees improve. They tend to be overly worried about getting along with people, often at the expense of the task at hand. This "anxious" type of affiliation has been found to drive down the climate rather than raise it. Stewing about whether they're liked or not, such leaders' avoidance of confrontation can derail a group, steering them to failure.[20]

Daniel Goleman

While most of the men and women we work with through Percept are highly moral people, we have been concerned with the overall lack of vision. Too often there is more concern for the survival of denominational structures and one's position within them than for faithfulness to the mission of the church. . . . But we wonder where the visionaries are.[21]

Mike Regele

Pastoral leadership, particularly in small rural areas, used to mean ministering to a small group of people, most of whom had a direct relationship with the pastor. Many churches carried this model into the urban environment and created the parish model of church life. Today, particularly in urban and suburban settings where the parish model has declined in relevance, pastors are finding that many of their constituents expect them to be visionaries and equippers. This new expectation implies that pastors will have significant relationships with only a small core of leaders rather than every person in the congregation. Many pastors have been caught in the transition between these models.

The vast majority of pastors, as a result of the traditional expectations of their constituents, are using a leadership style that could best be described as *participative* or *supportive*. They see themselves primarily as facilitators or consensus builders rather than genuine leaders. They see their job as doing a lot of listening and trying to make sure that everyone gets a hearing. To avoid dominating or being too authoritarian, they withhold their personal views or make sure they don't interject them until everyone else has had a chance to express their opinions. When these pastors do try to lead, most act as managers rather than leaders.

Another way of describing the typical leadership style of most pastors is to say it fits under a *chaplaincy* model of ministry. George Hunter, in his book *How to Reach Secular People*, estimates that at least eight out of ten churches operate out of this chaplaincy model, which he says is characterized by four basic assumptions:

- The primary ministry takes place inside the church, not outside in the world.
- The main object of ministry is believers, not nonbelievers.
- The ministry is the preserve of the clergy, not the laity.
- The validity of ministry is measured not by redeemed lives or changed communities but by vocational satisfactions of the clergy.

While the chaplain model has dominated the field of pastoral leadership, another model has gained some favor and attention over the last twenty years, particularly with the rise of the megachurch. Some pastors refer to it as the CEO model. In this model the pastor is viewed more like the head of a corporation or the chairman of the board. He is the focal point of all decision making, and the organization is clearly a top-down, leadership-driven model. Many of today's megachurches would fit this model, but clearly not all of them. Most pastors are passionately opposed to this model, and this would be expected from the vast majority who have adopted the chaplaincy model.

However, what is particularly interesting is that both models, while extremely different in the role and responsibility of the leader, have one thing in common. They both favor a lone-ranger approach to ministry. While both have responsibilities for a large number of people, they tend to carry out their ministry spending most of their time alone.

While we would have to admit that certain pastors seem to do well with either the chaplaincy model or the CEO model, I am not convinced this is the most appropriate model of ministry for most churches.

Behavioral Style

> From birth it is evident that people have certain God-given behavioral characteristics already in place that are basic and unique to their makeup.[22]
>
> Aubrey Malphurs

> It is my supposition that these temperaments are pre-packaged before birth and do not have to be cultivated or encouraged.[23]
>
> James Dobson

The topic of behavioral style has become quite popular in the last twenty years with the widespread use of the DISC, Myers-Briggs, and other similar type tests.[24] Most pastors and ministry leaders have taken one of these tests.

These instruments measure how we approach life, usually focusing on our work environment, and how we relate to others in that environment. The basic assumptions behind these tests, particularly as they relate to ministry, appear to be:

1. As leaders it is essential that we understand our behavioral style so that:

   a. We can understand how people read and interpret us—
      what signals we are sending through our conscious and
      subconscious behavior.
   b. We can use appropriate leadership strategies based
      on behavioral style. (As we lead we can emphasize the
      positive aspects of our behavioral style.)
   c. We can use appropriate strategies in working with
      others to enhance mutual effectiveness. (By knowing
      and recognizing the behavioral styles of others, we can
      understand the questions and concerns they might have
      and address those in a proactive way.)

2. There is no good or bad behavioral style.

   a. Mature or immature behavior is possible for all styles.
   b. What we all want is what Tim LaHaye labeled the "Spirit-
      controlled temperament."

3. Behavioral styles appear to be God-given, although in the process of conversion there may be adjustments.
4. Many differences that exist in the church are not theological
   or rational but rather the result of behavioral differences.
5. There is no "right" style for pastoral ministry. Any behavioral
   style can function in ministry. While some specialized roles in
   ministry might require certain behavioral styles, every style can
   function in harmony with other behaviors.
6. Every person has one dominant behavioral style from which
   he or she functions. Some will have a backup style that has above
   average strength and is used on occasion, but unless there is a
   conscious decision to do otherwise, people will normally function
   using their dominant behavioral style. An exception would be
   where, due to external pressures or job requirements, a person
   may consciously adjust his or her behavioral style for a season
   of time.

   Below you will find a diagram and descriptions that summarize the
DISC model for behavioral style. Note the letters *D*, *I*, *S*, and *C* in the
four quadrants, which stand for directness, influence, steadiness, and
competence. Each of these terms represent the chief attribute of each
behavioral style.

Task Oriented Product oriented Rational	C—Analyzer	Controller—D
People Oriented Process Oriented Emotional	S—Supporter	Promoter—I

Less Assertive/Verbal	More Assertive/Verbal
Tend to Respond	Tend to Initiate

Definitions of Behavioral Styles

The following are some of the positive and negative qualities of each of the behavioral styles in the DISC instrument. Remember that every style has positives and negatives. That is why one style is not "better" than another. People of every personality style can lead and influence others. Knowing our behavioral style(s) helps us better understand how we can and should lead.

HIGH D (CONTROLLER—DIRECTNESS)—LEAD BY VISION/CHALLENGE

POSITIVE QUALITIES	NEGATIVE QUALITIES
1. Imaginative and innovative 2. Excellent problem solvers 3. Self-confident 4. Like difficult tasks and challenges 5. Excellent at taking responsibility 6. Quick in thought and action 7. Persistent	1. Have extremely high expectations of others. Can become critical when their standards are not met 2. Often lack patience 3. Often lack empathy 4. Don't verbalize reasons for their conclusions

HIGH I (PROMOTER—INFLUENCE)—LEAD BY INSPIRATION

POSITIVE QUALITIES	NEGATIVE QUALITIES
1. Outgoing—interested in people 2. Develop friendships easily 3. Good promoters—enthusiastic 4. Optimistic 5. Excellent ability to verbalize 6. Confident	1. Often misjudge abilities of others 2. Often leap to overly favorable conclusions—overly optimistic 3. Have tough time controlling time schedules 4. Don't always use analytical data or get the facts they need 5. Too impulsive at times

HIGH S (SUPPORTER—STEADINESS)—LEAD BY RELATIONSHIP

POSITIVE QUALITIES	NEGATIVE QUALITIES
1. Empathetic—make people feel wanted and needed	1. Often do not assert themselves enough
2. Supportive—good listeners	2. Don't say no enough
3. Serve enthusiastically	3. Don't delegate enough
4. Calm and steady	4. Adapt slowly to change
5. Amiable and easygoing	5. Often need help in developing short-cut methods
6. Considerate and patient	
7. Consistent in their performance	

HIGH C (ANALYZER—COMPETENCE)—LEAD BY EXAMPLE/PLANNING

POSITIVE QUALITIES	NEGATIVE QUALITIES
1. Conscientious	1. May take a long time to make decisions and have trouble making them
2. Maintain and understand standards	2. Can get bogged down in details
3. Emphasize quality	3. Often feel they are judged more for what they do than who they are
4. Precise	4. Do not always share their feelings and opinions
5. Good at systematic thinking and planning	
6. Highly developed analytical abilities	

Some who have studied behavioral style have attempted to define the New Testament writers based on their temperaments or behavioral styles.[25] James has been called the apostle of the law or of works, Peter the apostle of hope, Paul the apostle of faith, and John the apostle of love. James has been assigned the phlegmatic temperament in its sanctified Christian state, Peter the sanguine, Paul the choleric, and John the melancholic. The four gospels also present similar differences, the first having close affinity to the position of James, the second to that of Peter, the third to that of Paul, and the fourth representing in its doctrinal element the spirit of John. While these are interesting speculations, the one conclusion that would have to be drawn is that God can use men and women of all behavioral or temperament types as effective leaders.

Behavioral Style in Ministry

While the numbers and percentages of people in each category of behavioral style vary depending on the group, generally speaking, there are significantly more "S" and "C" people than there are "D" and I."

However, in ministry, based on my empirical research, we have much larger percentages of pastors and ministry leaders who fall into the "High D" or "High I" categories than would normally be expected. The logical question is why? There are a couple of possible answers:

1. Because of the needs and demands of ministry, there is a higher demand for those with the more aggressive and verbal behavioral styles.
2. Pastors and ministry leaders have come to believe that the more aggressive behavioral styles are really "better" and act out those behaviors regardless of whether it is their true style.

My personal conclusion is that the second reason is much more common than many would think. It is very hard for people to avoid being influenced by the expectations and demands of those around them. In the same way we often form conclusions about what we would like to be or what we think we ought to be. Depending on our level of self-confidence and our place in God's training process, we may choose the option of acting in a way that is contrary to who we are and how we were designed by God, if we believe the situation requires it. Today's popular term for this is "dysfunctional." If a person forces himself to operate with a behavioral style that is contrary to his natural style, it is bound to create an inner tension and can be exhausting emotionally. There is an incredible freedom and peace when you can operate according to how you were designed by God.

But there is also confusion for those who are led by a dysfunctional leader. Invariably, the real behavioral style is bound to slip out, particularly when the leader is tired or under a lot of pressure. Those who follow such a leader have to decide which behavioral style is the "real" one. The normal response is simply to withdraw or try to avoid contact because of the possible misunderstandings and confusion.

What would be really odd and even more dysfunctional would be if pastors or ministry leaders as a whole really do have behavioral styles that are more aggressive and verbal than the average population. This would mean that they naturally initiate and prefer going in front. However, you will remember from above that the vast majority of pastors and ministry leaders are in fact using a leadership style that tells them not to initiate or go in front! In other words, if their natural behavioral style is on the aggressive, verbal side of the continuum, then it would be most natural for them to exhibit a leadership style that exhibited those characteristics. But they are not, which means one of two things:

- Leaders are trying to compensate for their behavioral style by using a leadership style that is much less aggressive.
- Leaders are trying to compensate for their real behavioral style by using another style that they feel is more suitable for the current situation.

Regardless of which is the case, it is unhealthy emotionally for pastors or ministry leaders, and equally unhealthy for the congregations they are trying to serve. To get out of this vicious cycle, you need to learn who you really are and begin to be comfortable with God's design for your life. Once you know your behavioral style, then you can learn how to best lead through that style. Every leader has to lead, to go in front, but how to do that varies a great deal based on one's behavioral style.

Summary

The issues surrounding leadership and behavioral styles discussed in this chapter are extremely important for pastors and ministry leaders. If leadership style is primarily a learned behavior, as many experts suggest, then it is particularly important for pastors and church leaders to understand their current leadership style and its strengths and weaknesses. If, as my research indicates, pastors and church leaders are primarily using leadership styles that are only minimally effective, the first step toward change must be understanding how we are presently trying to lead and how we can move toward a more effective leadership style.

If behavioral style is God-given, pastors and church leaders need to understand how God has wired them and what the implications are for ministry. This in itself will increase ministry effectiveness if it is moved from the subconscious to the conscious level of thinking. Once we fully understand the strengths and weaknesses of our behavioral style, we can minister more effectively in virtually any setting.

While leadership style and behavioral style are not the only critical issues related to Christian leadership, they are a great place to start.

Questions for Reflection

1. Would you agree that most Christian leaders you observe are not truly leaders? Why do you think this is true?
2. After reading the section on leadership style, which style do you think you most often use?
3. Have you heard of or been exposed to the adaptive or situational leadership model before? Why do you think it has become so popular, particularly in Christian circles, when there is very little research to support it?
4. After reading the section on behavioral style, which style do you think you are?
5. In the past how have you related leadership style with behavioral style?

2

WHY WE LACK EFFECTIVE CHRISTIAN LEADERSHIP

- THE DIFFERENCE BETWEEN LEADING AND MANAGING
- THE SERVANT-LEADER MODEL
- INAPPROPRIATE ORGANIZATIONAL DESIGN
- INEFFECTIVE SELECTION AND GOVERNANCE PROCESSES
- PASTORAL TURNOVER
- INADEQUATE LEADERSHIP TRAINING
- LEADERS GO ELSEWHERE
- FRUSTRATION WITH THE QUALITY OF PASTORAL LEADERSHIP
- NO PLAN FOR DEVELOPING MINISTRY LEADERS
- FALSE DICHOTOMY BETWEEN MINISTRY LEADERSHIP AND SECULAR LEADERSHIP
- SUMMARY

What do the words committees, elections, majority rule, boards, board members, parliamentary procedures, voting, and vote have in common? None of these words is found in the New Testament. We have imposed an American form of government on the church and, as a result, most churches are as bogged down in bureaucracy as our government is.[1]

Rick Warren

You cannot manage men into battle. You manage things; you lead people.[2]

Grace Murray Hopper

As important as the principles of servant leadership are, they do not display the full vista of the transforming Christian leadership that Jesus taught His disciples.[3]

Jerry Wofford

Their main leadership problem seemed to be that they did not believe their own stuff—not as it applies to the institutional affairs of their churches. They are able, conscientious persons, but they lack the kind of faith that anyone who would lead anything in a significant way must have.[4]

Robert K. Greenleaf

When the princes in Israel take the lead, when the people willingly offer themselves—praise the LORD!

Judges 5:2

R on was an outstanding pastor who founded and pastored his church for over twenty-five years. He was recognized as a pastor to pastors within his own church circles and had been very success-ful in restoring several pastors to ministry who had suffered from moral failure or personal burnout. He was recognized by most church members as an incredibly caring person who demonstrated genuine love, acceptance, and forgiveness, not just in the church but also in his personal life. His church had a solid reputation in the community, and many people who had suffered from church splits or conflict in other churches ended up attending Ron's church. However, a study of the growth history of the church showed a pattern of significant growth followed by significant decline. This cycle had repeated itself several times. As I worked with Ron as a consultant, I came to realize that being an outstanding pastor does not necessarily mean a person is also an excellent leader. This was particularly true in Ron's case. The root cause of the cycles of decline in his church was leadership failure, or at least leadership confusion.

Ron's case is not that unusual. I have seen this pattern in a majority of the churches I have worked with. Why does it happen? There is no simple answer to that question, but several factors are related to it. This chapter will examine some of these factors.

The Difference between Leading and Managing

Managing seeks to perpetuate the organization while promoting stability. Leading seeks to expand and develop an organization.[5]

Alan Nelson and Stan Toler

Management is fine as far as it goes, but leadership is the way to win.[6]

Noel Tichy and Stratford Sherman

There's a big difference between leading and managing. You can manage inventories, but you lead people. You can manage from afar, with a fax machine and a cellular phone, but you better be up close and personal when it comes to leading.[7]

Bill Parcells

People don't want to be managed. They want to be led.[8]

Warren Bennis and Burt Nanus

My personal observation is that most churches are overmanaged and underled. Many writers have defined the difference between leaders and managers, but the list below illustrates just some of the basic differences. While everyone involved in ministry or service will need to do both, it is the leadership practices that make the biggest difference. Warren Bennis has given the following distinctions between leadership and management:[9]

- The manager administers; the leader innovates.
- The manager maintains; the leader develops.
- The manager focuses on systems and structure; the leader focuses on people.
- The manager relies on control; the leader inspires trust.
- The manger has a short-range view; the leader has a long-range perspective.
- The manager asks how and when; the leader asks what and why.
- The manager accepts the status quo; the leader challenges it.
- The manger does things right; the leader does the right thing.

If you compared this list with the leadership style of the average pastor or ministry leader, it would be easy to see that there are a lot more managers than leaders.

The Servant-Leader Model

One of the reasons the participative or supportive style is so dominant among pastors and ministry leaders is because of their desire to fulfill what is termed the "servant-leader" model of leadership. The term "servant-leader" has been around for a long time but was popularized in 1977 when Robert Greenleaf wrote his book *Servant Leadership.*

While it is true that the biblical definition of a leader includes the injunction to "wash disciples' feet" and be willing to "lay down your life to protect the flock," this is only the servant side of the definition. There is another side that is equally important—leadership. Both are required to be a godly leader. The average pastor or church leader assumes leadership equals authoritarian control or the exercise of power, but these are not the marks of a true leader. To lead means to initiate, to walk in front or go before.

While most pastors and ministry leaders would define their leadership style as that of modeling the life of Jesus, they fail to understand the leadership style that Jesus really used. Jesus was willing to serve and give his life for his followers, but he also had a plan and a strategy for what he wanted to do with his disciples. His strategy was not to get up every morning, turn to his disciples, and say, "I have no idea of what we should do today, so what do you think? What would you like to do?" Jesus exemplified in perfect form how to be both a servant and a leader. Most pastors are trying to lead based on only the servant side of the servant-leader model. Why is that?

Most Pastors and Ministry Leaders Are Afraid to Lead

To get profit without risk, experience without danger, and reward without work is as impossible as it is to live without being born.[10]

Harry Truman

There's a fine line between delegating authority and turning the asylum over to the inmates. You want to be a fair, attentive, confident leader. You want to encourage people to take initiative, put forward original ideas, take the calculated risk. But if you go too far, you can wind up accommodating people. You can find yourself stepping back to keep the surface appearance of unity—and to avoid confrontation with people who are staging a house rebellion.[11]

Bill Parcells

We should not be surprised at this reluctance to lead when we remember the reluctance of many of God's chosen leaders such as Moses, Gideon, Saul, Jeremiah, and Esther when they were called.

When the angel of the Lord appeared to Moses, he was told, "So now, go, I am sending you to Pharaoh to bring my people the Israelites out of Egypt" (Exod. 3:10). Even though the Lord had spoken directly to him, Moses' response was a series of fearful questions.

- "Who am I, that I should go to Pharaoh and bring the Israelites out of Egypt?" (Exod. 3:11).
- "Suppose I go to the Israelites and say to them, 'The God of your fathers has sent me to you,' and they ask me, 'What is his name?' Then what shall I tell them?" (Exod. 3:13).
- "What if they do not believe me or listen to me and say, 'The LORD did not appear to you?'" (Exod. 4:1).
- "O Lord, I have never been eloquent, neither in the past nor since you have spoken to your servant. I am slow of speech and tongue" (Exod. 4:10). This is a particularly interesting statement by Moses. Look at what Stephen had to say about Moses in the book of Acts: "Moses was educated in all the wisdom of the Egyptians and was powerful in speech and action" (Acts 7:22).
- "O Lord, please send someone else to do it" (Exod. 4:13).

After all of these statements from Moses, Scripture records, "Then the LORD's anger burned against Moses" (Exod. 4:14). Moses certainly was not overly eager to lead the nation of Israel out of Egypt even though he was God's chosen instrument. Part of his reluctance may have been the result of a previous experience when he was rejected by his own people.

Gideon wasn't much better. The Lord told him, "Go in the strength you have and save Israel out of Midian's hand. Am I not sending you?" (Judg. 6:14). Gideon's responded by saying, "But Lord . . . how can I save Israel? My clan is the weakest in Manasseh, and I am the least in my family" (Judg. 6:15). The Lord promised to be with him, and still Gideon demanded a sign and later tested the Lord with a fleece.

Saul had all the natural qualities of a leader, but he was afraid to lead and depended completely on the prophet Samuel from the beginning. Even though Saul had been anointed by Samuel as the soon-to-be king, when they were ready to have the official consecration, Saul was found hiding in the baggage! Later when Saul failed to carry out the orders of Samuel in regard to the Amalekites, Samuel confronted Saul, saying, "Although you were once small in your own eyes, did you not become the head of the tribes of Israel? The LORD anointed you king over Israel" (1 Sam. 15:17).

When the Lord spoke to Jeremiah, he declared, "Before I formed you in the womb I knew you, before you were born I set you apart; I appointed you as a prophet to the nations" (Jer. 1:5). Jeremiah responded, "Ah, sovereign LORD, . . . I do not know how to speak; I am only a child" (Jer. 1:6).

Esther was asked by her cousin Mordecai "to go into the king's presence to beg for mercy and plead with him for her people" (Esther 4:8). Esther thought it was too dangerous and risky. Mordecai's response included the famous phrase "And who knows but that you have come to royal position for such a time as this?" (Esther 4:14). Esther replied that she would go: "I will go to the king, even though it is against the law. And if I perish, I perish" (Esther 4:16).

This pattern of reluctant leadership existed among God's chosen leaders in the past, so it should not surprise us to see it today. But shouldn't we profit from the wisdom of Scripture and avoid relearning these lessons the hard way?

Inappropriate Organizational Design

While most churches fail to realize it, they are organized so that pastors cannot lead. But why?

Because of Past Abuses of Power

The polity of the United Methodist Church, which is organized around distrust of individuals, makes it impossible for anyone to serve as the wagon master.[12]

Lyle Schaller

Many churches are trying to protect themselves from leadership abuse by making sure leaders cannot lead. As a result, they have regulated leadership into obscurity. The whole issue of authority has become confused with authoritarianism, and the baby has been thrown out with the bathwater. Let's face it, no church polity can totally eliminate the possibility of abuse of power. It is possible for the enemy to use people to circumvent the best church governmental systems and cause chaos and destruction in the church, so removing authority from pastors is not the answer to abuse. One church I worked with had a membership of 150 and a church board of 74, and most of the positions on the board were legislated by the denomination. Not surprisingly, the pastor found it difficult to get anything accomplished!

Because of Our Enamorment with the Democratic Process

The divisive effect of the vote is one which cannot be tolerated in the church, for the church is uniquely one. It cannot be forced to take sides and remain true to its nature. The vote approach to decision making must always do just this; it must force individuals to argue and attempt to convince, rather than help them work together to reach mutually agreeable solutions.[13]

F. F. Bruce

Most of America has become an extension of some committee. Well, you can't run a company as a democracy. It's more of a benevolent dictatorship. You set the direction and let people run.[14]

Ralph Burnett

A church is not just straightforward democracy, for in churches there is a common recognition of our fallen state, of our tendency to err, and, on the other hand, of the inerrancy of God's Word. So the members of a church congregation are democratic, perhaps, only in the sense that they work together as a congregation to try to understand God's Word.[15]

Mark Dever

The Bible teaches that the church is a family. In most family structures, the immature members (children) outnumber or at least equal the mature members (parents). In my family there are two parents and four children. If we voted on everything, we would have ice cream for dinner every night, never go to bed, and live at Disney World.[16]

James Emery White

Most U.S. churches operate as if the basic concepts of the democratic process are foundational biblical truths. They're not. Biblically, a better case can be made for casting lots than it can for voting.

Concepts such as checks and balances, parliamentary procedure, rule by the majority, and so forth are simply not biblical principles for churches. For example, a study of the Old and New Testament would show the majority of people were wrong far more times than they were right. Think of all the situations in the Old Testament where leaders had to deal with a majority that was definitely wrong. Moses and the prophets are prime examples. Unfortunately, not a great deal changed during New Testament times. Think of the exhortations Paul used with the churches he helped to start or the letters to the seven churches in the book of Revelation.

This is not to say there aren't principles in the democratic process that are biblical. This is also not to say that a church cannot or should not use democratic principles. However, the requirement that all decision making done in the church should meet the democratic principle or due-process test is wearing out leaders and congregations alike. The only way pastors can survive in these systems is to become astute politicians, carefully lobbying their views and making sure they get what they want passed. This is not the role God intended for his shepherds.

We need to recognize that the principles of a democratic system may very well be given by God, but that system is designed primarily to work in a world that is largely ungodly. It is not designed for the church. Remember in the Old Testament the people wanted a king like the other nations. That wasn't what God intended for them, but he allowed them to have a king to show them that the world's system of governance was not the true answer to their concerns.

Because of an overreliance on the democratic process, many churches have regulated away their vision. They have made it impossible for vision to be the driving force of the church. Instead, the church is driven by rules and policies. The result is ultimately a bureaucracy with endless meetings and committees to design more committees. The best people in the church end up being miniature politicians who *talk* about the work of the ministry but never have enough time to *do* the work of ministry. They may manage well, but they seldom lead.

Ineffective Selection and Governance Processes

Pastoral leadership is not the only kind of leadership missing in the church. Most people feel they have too few effective leaders throughout the church (e.g., elders, deacons, and board members). Churches are finding it harder and harder to recruit people for key leadership positions. Many of those who are filling these positions are tired and suffering from ministry fatigue.

The typical church uses some type of democratic process for choosing its elders, deacons, board members, and so on. However, this process breaks down in several areas.

- The average constituent doesn't know everyone in the congregation well enough to nominate someone or vote for a slate of candidates. Thus, the nomination process and the election process often end up being a popularity contest rather than a real choice based on biblical or leadership criteria. Thus, God's call and anointing is bypassed.
- The candidates that are put forward are usually representative of a small demographic segment of the church. If you look at most ministry leaders, you will see that they are significantly overrepresentative of older, long-term members. This gives a perception to people who are not in this group that they cannot play a significant role, and many look elsewhere to use their talents and gifts.
- The criteria for leadership are not clear to those who select the leaders. Most churches attempt to ensure that potential leaders meet biblical criteria, but even that poses problems. I remember an interesting discussion in one church where a potential leader met the biblical criteria but made it very clear that he did not like the direction the church was going and would do everything in his power to change that direction. Should that individual have been considered, or should he have been eliminated from con-

sideration? A significant controversy developed in the church, with groups forming on both sides of the issue.

- The actual commitment level of those who are chosen is often insufficient. Just one example is that many churches are surprised to find that many of their key leaders are not strongly committed to the church financially. Removing someone because of a lack of commitment is virtually impossible in most churches. The others in ministry leadership know that if they remove a person from leadership, regardless of the reasons, the fallout in the congregation will be severe, so they fail to deal with the issue.

Pastoral Turnover

Pastors of growing churches are generally characterized by longevity in the ministry.[17]

Peter Wagner

On average, today's pastors last only four years at a church and the average length of a pastoral career is just fourteen years—less than half of what it was not long ago.[18]

George Barna

A long pastorate does not guarantee a church will grow, but changing pastors every few years guarantees a church won't grow.[19]

Rick Warren

Several studies have indicated that the most fruitful years for pastors do not begin until their fourth or fifth years at a given church. And yet few pastors remain that long.

Carl George has pointed out an interesting phenomenon about pastoral turnover. In what he calls the Berry-Bucket theory, he showed that most churches go through a significant crisis somewhere between the fourth and sixth year of a new pastorate. This crisis may deal with a multiplicity of issues, but the underlying cause is the same in most cases—sociological issues dealing with the tenure and age of the pastor.

When the "new guard" approaches the "old guard" in voting power, a threat is perceived by the "old guard." Some time after four years, a congregation begins to realize that the minister's agenda for the future may contradict some of the long-time members' agendas. Lyle Schaller has described this tension as the classic conflict between the pioneers and the homesteaders.[20]

Most pastors when facing this crisis cannot understand the underlying pressure causing the turmoil and thus leave the church. The result is greater insecurity and fear on the part of people in the church. Subconsciously, many of the lay leaders say to themselves, "We must be the only true shepherds of this flock. These other guys come and go, but we are the only ones who remain with the flock, regardless of the circumstances." The pastors who come and go regularly are often viewed as "hirelings" or "wolves in sheep's clothing" who must be tolerated, not trusted, and who certainly should not be allowed to lead.

Unfortunately, many pastors are viewed this way. Recognize that much of this is subconscious among the leaders in the church. There is normally no conscious plan to keep the shepherd from leading. In fact, in most pastoral interviews, the lay leaders will express a real desire to be led by vision. However, when shepherds begin to lead, they encounter all kinds of resistance; the underlying cause is often unknown to everyone involved.

Thus, we see a vicious cycle of pastoral turnover that creates insecurity, fear, a lack of trust, and an unwillingness to allow pastoral leadership, which leads to more pastoral turnover.

This cycle must be broken if the church is to function as God intends. All sides need to face the issue openly and not give the enemy a foothold where he can cause apathy and dissension in the church.

Inadequate Leadership Training

Leadership is an art, not a science. . . . Assuming leadership duties without proper training, development, and experience can result in disastrous outcomes, for both the leader and the followers.[21]

George Barna

How do people learn to lead? How do they define their leadership style? Most empirical research indicates that we learn best by observing, by modeling, and through trial and error.

Unfortunately, most pastors and ministry leaders have never had the necessary training for four reasons.

- First, by far the majority of people have not grown up in churches where proper leadership was demonstrated, so they have seldom observed genuine Christian leadership.
- Second, few churches approach leadership development in an intentional way. That is, the number of churches who have a serious plan to recruit, mentor, train, deploy, and monitor future leaders is minimal. Thus, most pastors have not been involved in leadership training at the local church level.
- Third, pastors who have taken some type of formal training have basically experienced sit-and-soak learning where they were passive participants. They read books, listened to someone lecture about how to be a leader, and then tried to carry out whatever they had learned on their own.
- Fourth, pastors who have taken formal training receive very little training in the area of leadership.

Bible colleges and seminaries tend to blame the local church for failure to prepare Christian leaders, while the local churches tend to blame the training institutions. The truth is that both have failed. The training institutions have failed to apply the necessary educational philosophy and teaching strategies that ensure not just acquisition of knowledge but practical application. The churches have failed because most have no intentional plan to train leaders and provide the necessary practical experience.

A study that was done on companies that have won the prestigious Malcolm Baldrige National Quality Award showed that the average employee engaged in a staggering one hundred hours of training per year. Compare that with the average amount of annual training for pastors and ministry leaders.

We can see from the book of Acts that the early church focused on on-the-job training and mentoring as the primary ways to train and equip future ministry leaders. Those two keys are just as valuable today. But how often do we see them in action?

Leaders Go Elsewhere

People with leadership gifts, talents, or abilities have certain common traits that frustrate them when they attempt to work in typical ministry situations, as follows.

- **Leaders want to lead and accomplish something significant; they want to make an impact.** They want to feel that their contribution has made a difference. Unfortunately, in the church we relegate most good leaders to committees, where they are removed from the actual ministry of the church. They no longer do the work of the ministry; they simply talk about it.
- **Leaders tend to be driven or motivated by vision.** They want to know what it is they are trying to accomplish and why. They want to be sold on what they are doing and be passionate about it. Churches usually lack vision and don't have a clear focus. Therefore it is not unusual for many good Christian leaders to gravitate toward parachurch ministries, which tend to have a more clearly articulated vision, focus, and passion. Compare the quality of the average church board versus the average parachurch ministry board, and you will see the problem.
- **Leaders want to measure whether or not they are making a difference.** They want to know what "success" means in ministry, and they want to measure progress toward those ends. Churches normally do not define success and have rather vague definitions of what they are trying to accomplish. Thus, leaders find ministry leadership assignments very frustrating.
- **Leaders expect clear direction.** Oftentimes they are frustrated when they are asked to fulfill a ministry function and then find out the job description is vague or nonexistent. Most are asked to function without proper training or instruction, basically to fend for themselves. Their frustration often causes them to turn down future leadership opportunities in the church.

Frustration with the Quality of Pastoral Leadership

Potential ministry leaders often wrestle with another major issue—the leadership behavior or style of the pastor(s). Volunteers who are already working full-time do not want to come to meetings where the pastor demonstrates a lack of leadership. They cannot understand why those who are involved in the ministry of the church as a vocation do not initiate and define what is needed. As a result, leaders see the length of meetings increase and the quality of results decline.

The net result for these leaders is a general frustration and a decision to use their time elsewhere. Because they love and respect the pastor(s), they do not want to cause a problem and normally never discuss their real frustrations, and as a result, everyone loses.

No Plan for Developing Ministry Leaders

Few churches have a clear plan for how to train leaders. As a result, they try to look for someone who is already a leader or someone who has led somewhere else. These are not always the best people, and it prevents the development of new leaders.

A study of the early church in the book of Acts and in the letters of Paul indicates there was a very intentional process of developing leaders. The discipleship process of Jesus and later Paul indicates how serious early Christians were about producing leaders. The people they selected were not all natural leaders and they made plenty of mistakes, but the process eventually produced the necessary leaders. Churches would do well to rethink this critical area.

How many times have we heard the admonition as Christian leaders to fulfill the assignment given to us in Ephesians 4:11–13?

> It was he who gave some to be apostles, some to be prophets, some to be evangelists, and some to be pastors and teachers, to prepare God's people for works of service, so that the body of Christ may be built up until we all reach unity in the faith and in the knowledge of the Son of God and become mature, attaining to the whole measure of the fullness of Christ.

It is clear from this passage that one of our primary responsibilities as Christian leaders is to prepare or equip God's people. In order to do that we must be proactive and intentional. And we must dedicate the necessary time. The discipling process we see in the lives of Jesus and Paul was not a part-time thing. It was at the core of their ministry. How many pastors can truly say that about their current ministry?

False Dichotomy between Ministry Leadership and Secular Leadership

Unfortunately, the teaching and philosophy in many churches is that we must totally separate ministry leadership from leadership in the world. This means rejecting any concept or idea that is "secular." The result is that many godly leaders who work in the business world and who have developed their leadership skills over many years feel constrained from using these skills or providing leadership in the church. They feel that what they have to offer is not "biblical leadership."

And the church feels the same way. While they don't have a clear understanding of what "biblical leadership" means, they know they must reject anything that has a hint of the secular in it, so anyone who is a business leader is deemed a threat to the purity of the "Christian leadership" model. While it might not be stated in such stark terms, the assumptions are definitely there. Many pastors are concerned about what they see as the CEO leadership model for pastors. They say this model defines ministry success or effectiveness by numbers of people, dollars, and buildings. What intrigues me as a consultant is when I ask people with these views how they measure success and what information they track regularly in their churches, invariably they will say they keep track of attendance and income!

The Scriptures do not seem to make this dichotomy between secular and church leadership. The Christian is required to live consistently with the principles of Scripture regardless of whether he or she is in the church or in the business community. Nowhere is it suggested or implied that there should be a difference in how the Christian leads depending on the circumstance.

We can agree that many business leadership principles are used in the world that do not meet the test of Scripture. On the other hand, many things learned in the process of business do meet the scriptural test and can be fully used in the business world as well as in the business of the church.

Summary

The factors identified in this chapter help explain why we have so much confusion in the church regarding Christian leadership and why we see so few good models in our churches. It may have surprised you how many factors are working against effective Christian leadership. However, none of these is irreversible. None of them has to become permanent features of an individual's life or of the church they serve.

We would be wise to reexamine our own lives and identify the personal and environmental factors that have significantly limited our Christian leadership potential. Once we know what we are up against, we can begin thinking about how we can initiate change. Every biblical leader had to wrestle with both personal and corporate issues that potentially limited his or her leadership effectiveness. We have examples of men and women chosen by God who failed to deal adequately with personal or corporate obstacles and were derailed in the process. We have many more examples, however, of leaders who overcame these obstacles and significantly impacted their world for God.

Questions for Reflection

1. Is your leadership style more like that of a manager or a leader?
2. Has your understanding of the "servant-leader" model of leadership been helpful or harmful in your ministry? Why?
3. Is your church organized so that pastors can really lead and provide vision?
4. Do you believe the selection and governance processes you are currently using in your church are helping or hindering genuine leadership? Why?
5. Review the formal training you have received regarding leadership. Has it been inadequate? If so, why do you think that is true?
6. Do you believe key lay leaders in your church are frustrated by the pastoral leadership? If so, why?
7. Do you have an intentional plan in your church to develop leaders?
8. Does your church suffer from a false dichotomy between ministry leadership and secular leadership?

3

MINISTRY LEADERSHIP AND ORGANIZATIONAL STRUCTURE

- JEWISH LEADERSHIP AND ORGANIZATIONAL STRUCTURE
- NEW TESTAMENT LEADERSHIP AND ORGANIZATIONAL STRUCTURE
- SUMMARY

We are almost wholly dependent on the Letters of Paul for our knowledge of the spread of Christianity beyond Jerusalem, and what information he provides—welcome though it is—is limited in scope, since it obviously concentrates on his own experiences and associations. Nevertheless this is the most important historical source we have, and it must be examined with care if we are to understand how the Church grew beyond its Jewish setting to become an inclusive community.[1]

Howard Clark Kee, Franklin W. Young, and Karlfried Froehlich

The NT provides no detailed code of regulations for the government of the church, and the very idea of such a code might seem repugnant to the liberty of the gospel dispensation; but Christ left behind him a body of leaders in the apostles whom he himself had chosen, and he also gave them a few general principles for the exercise of their ruling function.[2]

The New Bible Dictionary

Bill's church found itself at a very difficult juncture. Although the church had grown and established itself in its community, there seemed to be an underlying tension that was growing both inside and outside the leadership circle. Over the last three years there had been several issues of conflict in the church. The pastor and board of the church had done their best to deal with the problems, but it seemed as if they would get one issue dealt with only to discover another major issue on the horizon. Bill could not figure out what was going on. The board and lay leaders were equally concerned. At any given time it seemed like the issue they dealt with was not the real issue behind the conflict, but they could not figure out the reason for the conflict. Despite several congregational meetings and multiple meetings where the leadership team attempted to define the problems, nothing seemed to provide the real answer.

One evening at the monthly board meeting, Larry's church board got into a discussion about church leadership and organizational structure. Some of the members criticized the church's government structure, and they were asking the board to reorganize the church around a more biblical pattern. As Larry and the elders began to discuss this issue, they realized that there was not even a consensus among themselves regarding these issues. Many in the room had come from other churches, and the leadership and organizational structure in each of these churches had been somewhat different from the next. Was there such a thing as a biblical pattern? If so, what was it?

Bill's church and Larry's church were facing issues that many churches in the United States are dealing with today. These issues regard leadership and organizational structure. Over time Christian churches have developed many different structures and nomenclature for the persons who fill the leadership roles. As a result, there is much confusion about what ministry leadership structure should look like. Surprisingly, despite the many differences, most denominations and most churches have accepted the pastor/staff/board model as the standard leadership design.

The best place to begin when discussing leadership and organizational structure is to look at the early church as it is described in Scripture. From what we see in the book of Acts and the Pastoral Epistles, we can draw several conclusions about leadership structure.

- Church structure was an evolving concept over a number of years. As the church grew and developed, the leadership structure changed according to a number of different factors.
- Not surprisingly, the earliest forms of ministry leadership followed Jewish patterns. Since the earliest Christians had Jewish backgrounds of one kind or another, they naturally used the forms that they were used to. Even the format of services in the churches followed quite closely the format in the synagogues.
- Christians predominantly gathered in home congregations that were relatively small, the largest probably not exceeding one hundred people. On certain occasions and depending on the availability of facilities, the congregations in a city gathered together for joint meetings.
- All of the churches described in the New Testament were citywide churches with multiple congregations. Early Christians interacted predominantly within a small group of people in a home group, but in the New Testament the term "church" refers to all the believers in a city. Many people have been confused by this because we use the word in a different way today. Certainly because of the geographical proximity and the size of those cities, Christians from different home congregations knew and related to one another in natural settings. Using the Jerusalem church as an example, however, a church often had several thousand believers, which is quite a different picture than that of an American church today, where the average church has about 150 people.
- It appears these early churches were basically divided along cultural lines. This means that in primarily Jewish congregations some were mainly Aramaic-speaking Hebrew Christians, while others were predominantly Greek-speaking Hebrew Christians. Other congregations were composed primarily of Gentiles (non-Jewish believers).

Jewish Leadership and Organizational Structure

Jewish leadership structure focused on three primary elements: (1) the local synagogue, (2) the Sanhedrin, and (3) the temple in Jerusalem.

In the Scriptures the synagogue was a gathering of individuals in a local area for worship, instruction, and prayer. A city, depending on its size, could have several synagogues. Jerusalem had approximately four hundred synagogues in AD 70. The synagogue was led by elders, the number of which seemed to vary based on the size of the synagogue. These elders appear to have been appointed to their positions. Each synagogue was led by one of the elders who was called the "leader" or "ruler" (Mark 5:22; Acts 13:15; 18:8). This leader was considered a "first among equals," meaning that he had leadership authority but certainly was not autocratic. Each synagogue also had "attendants" or servants who helped carry out the activities of the synagogue.

The Sanhedrin was a council of elders and priests (Matt. 5:22; 10:17; Mark 13:9; Acts 22:5) who likely ruled over a city or a regional area. Because the temple was in Jerusalem, the Sanhedrin there became the key ruling body for the Jewish people. It was led by the high priest who presided over all meetings.

The temple was the heart of Jewish religious life, but except for those living in Jerusalem, it did not have the influence over the daily life of most Jewish people that the synagogue or local councils did.

New Testament Leadership and Organizational Structure

As mentioned already, it appears that the early Christian church borrowed liberally from the Jewish structures.

- The citywide churches had elders who were appointed and provided leadership. The individual congregations, depending on the size, had one or more elders.
- The churches had deacons or ministers who helped carry out the ministry of the churches.
- The churches had an order of service that was very similar in format to that which took place in the synagogues.

However, some different elements also shaped the leadership structure. The early church had the disciples of Jesus (eventually termed apostles) to help guide and shape their structure and organization. These apostles also played a major role in the development of the churches outside of Jerusalem, particularly in Samaria and Antioch.

Interestingly, we find within a very short time James, the brother of Jesus, who was not even a believer when Jesus was on the earth, is described as an apostle and leader of the church in Jerusalem (Acts 15:13; 21:18; Gal. 2:9, 12).

Peter and John, who were two of the three people closest to Jesus during his earthly ministry, were also two of the most important leaders in the early church (Gal. 2:2, 9). It was Peter and John who were sent to Samaria to validate the work done by Philip the Evangelist. It was Peter who had the vision recorded in Acts 10 and then was obedient in going to the house of Cornelius (a Gentile), making Peter the first Jew in the New Testament to preach to Gentiles.

Paul became the other major leader, particularly in the expansion of Christianity to the Gentiles throughout the Mediterranean area. The ministry leaders in Jerusalem formally recognized Paul's leadership role in ministering to the Gentiles, while Peter was identified as the one to lead those of Jewish heritage to Christianity. Although he was not one of the disciples of Jesus and had even joined in the persecution of early Christians, Paul was declared an apostle because of his dramatic encounter with Christ on the road to Damascus and the commissioning he received to preach to the Gentiles. It appears that the other apostles did not dispute this title. Paul writes to the Galatians:

> On the contrary, they saw that I had been entrusted with the task of preaching the gospel to the Gentiles, just as Peter had been to the Jews. For God, who was at work in the ministry of Peter as an apostle to the Jews, was also at work in my ministry as an apostle to the Gentiles. James, Peter and John, those reputed to be pillars, gave me and Barnabas the right hand of fellowship when they recognized the grace given to me. They agreed that we should go to the Gentiles, and they to the Jews. All they asked was that we should continue to remember the poor, the very thing I was eager to do.
>
> Galatians 2:7–10

The church in Antioch became the base for Paul as he was invited to be part of the ministry there by Barnabas. Barnabas, whom Paul termed an apostle (Acts 14:4, 14; 1 Cor. 9:3–6), had been sent by the church in Jerusalem both to validate the work there and to help them in their development. The church at Antioch was filled primarily with Gentiles, many of whom were loosely associated with Judaism and were called God-fearers. The two early churches were quite different in composition, the church in Jerusalem being primarily people with Jewish heritage and the church in Antioch primarily Gentiles.

Thus, we see the apostles superintending the development of the early churches. Their ministry was one whereby they traveled from church to church. These apostles were recognized as having authority in the churches, but it appears in many cases that when they were in a local church, they submitted to the leadership there. It's logical that they would be recognized as authorities by virtue of their ministry with Jesus, or in Paul's case because of his founding role in the Gentile churches. It appears that they exercised their leadership roles primarily by influencing others, not just by using authority based on their spiritual office.

Ministry Leadership Structure as Defined by the Apostle Paul

Paul provides two primary passages that define ministry leadership.

It was he who gave some to be apostles, some to be prophets, some to be evangelists, and some to be pastors and teachers, to prepare God's people for works of service, so that the body of Christ may be built up until we all reach unity in the faith and in the knowledge of the Son of God and become mature, attaining to the whole measure of the fullness of Christ.

Ephesians 4:11–13

And in the church God has appointed first of all apostles, second prophets, third teachers, then workers of miracles, also those having gifts of healing, those able to help others, those with gifts of administration, and those speaking in different kinds of tongues.

1 Corinthians 12:28

From these lists we can determine several things:

- There appears to be an order of offices for church leadership. While we do not see this "chain of authority" being carried out in an autocratic manner, it does appear that it represented an order based on influence or significance.
- These offices were recognized across the spectrum of Christian churches.

- These offices did not operate independently of one another but in genuine partnership to carry out God's will through the churches.
- The primary purpose of these offices was for the training and equipping of God's people and particularly for the training and equipping of leaders for the churches.

Apostles

It seems natural to us that the apostles are first on the list. Having either ministered directly with Jesus or having had some kind of personal encounter with Christ, we would expect them to have authority and influence. The role of these apostles was to provide the foundation for the churches. Normally these apostles had an itinerant or traveling ministry.

In the New Testament we find several people who are designated "apostles" other than the original twelve (see Acts 14:14; Rom. 16:7; Gal. 1:19; 2:9; 1 Thess. 2:6). This would seem to imply that the office of apostle went significantly beyond the original twelve, although some argue that it did not go beyond the seventy who were sent out by Jesus.

By the second century we no longer see apostles written about by the early Christian writers. Instead, the single bishop system was emerging. This system had one person in full authority for a particular geographic area. This change and whether it was what God intended is open to debate. It may have emerged as a response to some of the heretical movements that arose shortly after the church began, or it may have simply been an issue of control. We will never know the answer, but the term "apostle" no longer appears by the time of the second century.

Today some see a reemergence of the role and function of apostles and link it either to church planting or church governance, regardless of whether they are formally called apostles. Others are more adamant about the significance of the title itself. But clearly there is no agreement across the Christian spectrum on the role of apostles today.

Prophets

Why prophets are second in the lists is somewhat more puzzling, although two reasons seem to stand out.

- Prophets were a critical part of Jewish history, recognized as agents of God who spoke words of wisdom, encouragement, and exhortation. When the Christian church started, prophets were a natural part of the transition.
- Some prophets also had itinerant or traveling ministries and thus were not always tied to a local church or geographical location.

Prophets played a vital role in the early church well into the second century. After that there seems to be growing concern about how to mix the itinerant ministry of the prophets and their presumed authority with the local ministry of the bishops and elders.

It appears from a reading of the New Testament that the authority of the prophets was primarily spiritual and often involved teaching. Prophets sometimes prophesied future events but more often spoke through words of revelation for the edification of the church.

Once the single bishop system came into being, the role of the prophets decreased significantly, particularly as it related to local church ministry.

Today we see a new debate emerging in the church regarding prophets. It follows the same lines of thinking regarding spiritual gifts. Some have argued that the roles and gifts of apostles and prophets ceased with the canonization of Scripture. However, others strongly dispute this view. As the *New Bible Dictionary* states, "There appears to be no good reason why the living God, who both speaks and acts (in contrast to the dead idols), cannot use the gift of prophecy to give particular local guidance to a church, nation or individual, or to warn or encourage by way of prediction as well as by reminders, in full accord with the written word of Scripture, by which all such utterances must be tested."[3]

We can only speculate whether this is what God intended, or whether man's need for control actually stopped what God was trying to do. We do know one thing: prophets were recognized as a legitimate part of the church well into the second century.

Evangelists

Why evangelists are third in the Ephesians list is even more difficult to understand because this was not a common term or office. However, the meaning is clearly "one who brings good news." The noun form of this is found only three times in the New Testament (Acts 21:8; Eph. 4:11; 2 Tim. 4:5), although the verb form is used throughout the New

Testament. We know that the apostles carried out the work of evangelism, proclaiming the Christian gospel to those who had not heard, but
there were others who did this as well. Philip is specifically called an
evangelist in Acts 21:8, and we see his ministry clearly described and
defined with the Samaritans and with the Ethiopian in Acts 8. The
evangelists may be listed just after the prophets because they too
were involved in itinerant ministry. The role of the evangelists was to
share the gospel message to others in groups or one-on-one and to
help found churches for new believers.

Pastors/Teachers

Fourth in the Ephesians list is pastors or pastors/teachers. Third in
the 1 Corinthians list is teachers. There is some debate as to whether
this is supposed to be two offices or one. Both refer to offices that are
associated with specific local churches and whose function was to serve
the needs of the local congregation. From Acts 20 and 1 Peter 5 we
can assume that the terms "pastor," "shepherd," "overseer," "bishop,"
"presbyter," and "elder" are used interchangeably although there may
be distinctions in particular biblical passages.

These leaders were evidently appointed, either by the apostles and
prophets (Acts 14:23) or by the leaders of the citywide church with the
laying on of hands (1 Tim. 4:14; 5:22; 2 Tim. 1:6). They were commonly
recognized as the leaders of the churches and congregations (Acts
20:17–35; Phil. 1:1; 1 Tim. 4:14; 5:17, 19; Titus 1:5). Whether there were
multiple elders in every congregation is open to some question, but we
know at least that there were multiple elders in each city. These elders
met together on occasions and someone in the group was recognized
as the leader, probably based on the format of the Sanhedrin in the
Jewish system. This leader served as president of a college of fellow
elders and thus was viewed as a "first among equals."

The role of the pastors/teachers was to guide, instruct, feed, and
provide pastoral care and oversight for a specific flock of God.

Ministry Leadership Structure in Jerusalem and Antioch

We do not have any description of the leadership structure of the
church in Jerusalem other than the fact that it was led by apostles and
elders, with James, the brother of Jesus, as the acting "president." What

we have regarding the church in Antioch is also minimal but somewhat more descriptive than in Jerusalem. In Acts 13 the leadership is described as follows: "In the church at Antioch there were prophets and teachers: Barnabas, Simeon called Niger, Lucius of Cyrene, Manaen (who had been brought up with Herod the tetrarch) and Saul. While they were worshiping the Lord and fasting, the Holy Spirit said, 'Set apart for me Barnabas and Saul for the work to which I have called them.' So after they had fasted and prayed, they placed their hands on them and sent them off" (Acts 13:1–3).

We know that two of these leaders, Paul and Barnabas, were also called apostles. Thus, the leadership team at Antioch was composed of apostles, prophets, and teachers. This squares with what Paul wrote about the leadership offices in Ephesians 4 and 1 Corinthians 12 and implies a collegial approach to ministry in the church.

The Council of Jerusalem

When a dispute arose in Antioch about the membership requirements for non-Jewish believers, it was settled at the Council of Jerusalem (Acts 15). Evidently some men had come from Judea to Antioch and were demanding that the Gentile converts submit to circumcision in order to become genuine Christians. Paul and Barnabas disagreed with them and were sent by the church in Antioch to get the opinion of the leaders in Jerusalem. From Acts 15 we can make the following conclusions:

- The church in Antioch looked to the church in Jerusalem for input and support.
- Those who headed this council were the apostles and elders (Acts 15:6). This council thus reminds us of the Jewish Sanhedrin and its format.
- The council was headed by James, the brother of Jesus. Scripture clearly indicates that James was not only the recognized leader but took the initiative in leading the council to a decision. This again fits the pattern of the Sanhedrin with one person having leadership responsibility among equals.
- There was a significant association between the church in Antioch and the church in Jerusalem. As a result, there was a serious effort to provide unity on the basics of the faith for both Jewish and Gentile believers.

Summary

What conclusions can we draw from the history of the early church regarding leadership and organizational structure?

- A great deal of freedom was allowed in determining ministry leadership structure and organization. Churches were not required to have the same structure. Contextual needs helped shape church structures and organization. The church in Jerusalem with its strong Jewish background and involvement of the first apostles was organized and operated differently than the church in Antioch with its primarily Gentile background. And the church in Antioch with leaders such as Paul and Barnabas was organized and operated differently than the churches planted by Paul in his missionary journeys.
- The early church believed in a multiplicity of leaders in a church or a team approach to ministry. Remember, when the New Testament uses the term "church," it is referring to all the Christians in a city with many small congregations meeting throughout that city. Different terms were used for these leaders, but "elders" is probably the most common usage.
- The early church recognized the importance of multiple gifts within the leadership team of a local congregation as well as of the citywide church.
- Every leadership team (in the local congregation or the citywide church) had one recognized leader who was considered a "first among equals." Thus, they could not lead in an autocratic or dictatorial manner but led by influence.
- The early church allowed primarily itinerant ministries (apostles, prophets, and evangelists) to play a significant role, particularly in the development of new churches. The established churches looked to these itinerant ministers for advice, counsel, and exhortation in regard to local church ministry. Local ministry leadership submitted to the wisdom and influence of these traveling leaders and viewed their role as critical to the development of old and new churches alike. The apostles, prophets, and evangelists were known by the local ministry leadership and were well tested to verify the validity of their ministries.
- Early ministry leaders believed in the continual training and development of new leaders. Those with traveling ministries always

took other potential leaders along with them and discipled them with on-the-job training. Local leaders also believed in multiplying effective leaders. The fivefold ministry described in Ephesians 4 was given for the purpose of equipping others, not just providing leadership.

The early church gives us some patterns and guidance as we seek to provide biblical leadership in the church today. The foundations laid by the early New Testament ministry leaders provide significant direction as we seek to define Christian leadership for today. One thing that is abundantly clear is that God allowed a great deal of flexibility in regard to leadership and organizational structure while maintaining complete unity in the church, as alluded to in this excerpt from *The New Bible Dictionary*:

> The general pattern of church government in the apostolic age would seem to be a board of elders or pastors, possibly augmented by prophets and teachers, ruling each of the local congregations, with deacons to help, and with a general superintendence of the entire church provided by apostles and evangelists.[4]

Questions for Reflection

1. Do you agree with the general outline given in this chapter regarding church leadership and organizational leadership in the first century? Why or why not?
2. Do you agree with the general principles given in this chapter regarding the apostle Paul's definition of Christian leadership? Why or why not?
3. What is your personal conviction regarding the role of apostles, prophets, evangelists, and pastors/teachers in the church today?
4. Do you agree with the general principles given in the summary regarding Christian leadership in the early church? Why or why not?

4

DEFINING LEADERSHIP

- ■ ARE LEADERS BORN OR MADE?
- ■ SECULAR LEADERSHIP THEORY
- ■ BIBLICAL LEADERSHIP THEORY
- ■ DIFFERENCES BETWEEN SECULAR AND BIBLICAL LEADERSHIP THEORY
- ■ SUMMARY

Leadership is not an exclusive club for those who were "born with it." The traits that are the raw materials of leadership can be acquired.[1]

John Maxwell

Leadership is the ability to elicit extraordinary performance from ordinary people.[2]

Brian Tracy

Spiritual leadership is moving God's people on to God's agenda.[3]

Henry Blackaby and Richard Blackaby

No one need aspire to leadership in the work of God who is not prepared to pay a price greater than his contemporaries and colleagues are willing to pay. True leadership always exacts a heavy toll on the whole man, and the more effective the leadership is, the higher the price to be paid.[4]

J. Oswald Sanders

L es was considered a very successful pastor within his denomination and by the students at the local seminary where he often taught classes. However, his church had recently gone through an extremely difficult situation regarding moral failure on the part of one of the assistant pastors in the church. As often happens, the church was visibly split over what should be done. Some wanted the pastor to remain in the church, to be counseled and hopefully restored to ministry in the future. Others wanted severe public church discipline to be directed against the offending pastor. Les tried to lead the church through this difficult time, but the net result was a loss of almost one-third of the church. Les was so discouraged that he almost gave up his ministry. However, as I began to work with Les and his church, he rediscovered his passion for ministry and redefined a very compelling vision for the church, and less than a year later the church was not only back on its feet but paid off their entire debt in one offering as a sign of their commitment to the future.

Before going further we must define what we mean by "leadership" and in particular what we mean by "Christian leadership." But even before we do that we need to answer an age-old question, "Are leaders born or made?"

Are Leaders Born or Made?

There is certainly plenty of evidence to support both positions. It very well may be that there are some innate characteristics that are passed on genetically that make leadership a more natural behavior. We also have to admit that certain individuals have significant advantages from the environment in which they are raised and nurtured. There is also a biblical gift of leadership; some people are supernaturally endowed by God with special leadership abilities. In addition, as we saw in the previous chapter, Ephesians 4 lists a number of offices for which certain people seem to be supernaturally gifted.

But what about the vast majority of us who are not genetically endowed with great leadership skill, did not grow up in environments that nurtured leadership ability, do not have the biblical gift of leadership, and are not called to one of the offices in Ephesians 4. Is there any hope?

And even for those who have leadership gifts or offices, can leadership skills be developed or enhanced for more effective leadership?

The answer to these questions is a resounding yes! Everyone can increase his or her leadership ability through focused and active learning. For most leadership environments, including those in the church, this is more than enough to provide the necessary leadership traits and behaviors.

For encouragement, note the following comments:

> But for those who are not born leaders, or those who do not have the gift of leadership, it appears that they can learn certain leadership behaviors that will significantly increase their effectiveness. This is going to be true for most that find themselves in leadership positions. It is not the exception, but the norm. And even those with innate leadership abilities or those with the gift of leadership can improve their leadership ability through study and practice. Effective leadership does not come easily to anyone, but it can be learned.[5]

> Robert Logan

> "Are leaders born or made?" It's a judgment call. No one knows for sure. Our experience tells us that leadership is a set of learnable competencies. We can, however, tell you this for certain: every exceptional leader we know is also a learner.[6]

> James M. Kouzes and Barry Z. Posner

Secular Leadership Theory

There certainly is no shortage of definitions or descriptions of what secular writers believe regarding leadership. Here are just a few samples:

> Leadership is the capacity and will to rally men and women to a common purpose and the character which inspires confidence.[7]

> Bernard Montgomery, British Field Marshal

> Leaders are people who perceive what is needed and what is right and know how to mobilize people and resources to accomplish mutual goals.[8]

> Thomas E. Cronin

The art of leadership: liberating people to do what is required of them in the most effective and humane way possible.[9]

Max DePree

Leadership is the art of getting someone else to do something you want done because he wants to do it.

Dwight D. Eisenhower

Over the years several secular theories of leadership have developed.

- The first was what became known as the *universal traits* or "great men" theory. This theory focused on the characteristics or traits that leaders exhibit. This empirical research started by identifying so-called great men and then tried to categorize what qualities were common among them. The primary assumption behind this theory was that there must be common traits or characteristics of great leaders. While the early research assumed this was just a natural part of certain individuals (either the product of genes or environment), later adaptations allowed for the possibility of learned traits that would improve anyone's leadership ability.
- The second became known as the *universal behavior* theory. This theory focused on what leaders did—what behaviors they exhibited. The initial description of this theory was to place leadership behavior along a single continuum ranging from *people-oriented* leadership (strong focus on relationships and feelings) at one extreme and *task-oriented* leadership (strong focus on tasks or outcomes) at the other. This later changed to a two-dimensional grid with people orientation as one variable and task orientation as the other.
- The third was labeled *contingency traits* theory. This theory assumed that there was no universal set of traits that would work in every setting and that leadership must depend at least in part on the situation or context. Another assumption behind this theory was that leaders basically exhibit common traits over their lifetime. Thus, matching the appropriate leader to the appropriate situation offered the best hope for effective leadership. However, this implied that as a group's situation changed over time (a natural occurrence), the group would need different leaders.
- The fourth was labeled *contingency behavior* theory. This theory is similar to the last one in that it focuses on situational or contextual issues. However, it assumes that the leader is able to adapt

his behaviors based on the needs of the situation. Here, analyzing the situation focused on the task relevant maturity of those being led. Task-relevant maturity was defined as *job maturity*—competence or ability to do a job—and *psychological maturity*, which is the confidence or willingness to do a job. Another assumption of this theory is that as the group matures (i.e., becomes more familiar, comfortable, and capable with the task), the effective leader provides less and less directive behavior and eventually less relationship behavior, so the group is assuming more and more responsibility for itself.

In recent years two additional theories have been added to the four general theories above.

- The first has been labeled an *open systems* approach. Systems thinking became popular with the writings of Peter Senge and his associates at the Sloan School of Management, Massachusetts Institute of Technology (MIT). Systems thinking assumes that the leadership process is a system of multiple variables in which each set of variables is influenced by and in turn influences numerous other sets of variables.[10] These variables include input variables (traits and behaviors of the leader as well as the group) and output variables (satisfaction and group performance).

Even with the preferred personality traits and interpersonal skills in hand, the transformational leader or would-be change agent must also appreciate the dynamic, systemic forces that are already present in the organization in which he or she serves. Without that knowledge or the tools to modify these forces (or patterns of events) toward intended goals, even the leader who is naturally gifted and trained for transformation may fail in his or her efforts to bring lasting organizational change.[11]

Alan McMahan

- Another popular theory has been labeled *transformational* leadership. Popularized by James McGregor Burns and later by Bernard Bass, this theory suggests that effective leaders are people who initiate change by motivating people to do more than they expected they could do, increasing awareness of different values, and getting people to go beyond their self-interests to a higher good or cause. In this theory the effective leader is a person who helps followers to change, to move from where they are to where they should be or where they really want to be. The key components of transformational leadership as defined by Bass include: (1) Idealized Influence or Charisma (providing vision and sense of mission, instilling pride, and gaining respect and trust), (2) Inspiration or Inspirational Motivation (communicating high expectations, using symbols to focus efforts, expressing important purposes in simple ways), (3) Intellectual Stimulation (promoting intelligence, rationality, and careful problem solving), and (4) Individualized Consideration (giving personal attention, treating each follower individually, coaching, or advising).

What conclusions can we draw from all these theories about leadership? The most obvious is that leadership is a very complex process, involving many variables. The degree of importance of each of these variables is what seems to be in dispute.

Second, while almost everyone can agree on what a great leader is when they see one, we find it much more difficult to explain how or why a person is a great leader.

Third, it appears that the early theories were overly simplistic in their attempts to define leadership. While they helped define some of the variables, the theories were incomplete.

Biblical Leadership Theory

There has been a corresponding search among Christian sources to define leadership within a biblical or scriptural context. Here are some definitions from various Christian writers:

A biblical leader is defined as a person with God-given capacity and God-given responsibility to influence a specific group of God's people toward His purposes for the group.[12]

Robert Clinton

Transforming leaders are those who are able to divest themselves of their power and invest it in their followers in such a way that others are empowered, while the leaders themselves end with the greatest power of all, the power of seeing themselves reproduced in others.[13]

Leighton Ford

The main verb Paul used to describe the Christian leader's job in Ephesians 4:12, "to prepare," is the same Greek word sometimes translated "to equip," which literally means "to put in working order" or "to repair." It is used in the classical Greek in reference to setting a broken bone and, in the Gospels, to mend a torn net.[14]

Robert Logan

Empowering leadership is the process of helping others to recognize strengths and potential within, as well as encouraging and guiding the development of these qualities. . . . Empowering leadership is the affirmation of another's ability to learn and grow and become all that they are meant by God to be mature in Christ.[15]

Jack Balswick and Walter Wright

Leadership is the ability to obtain followers.[16]

John Maxwell

Probably the best place to start in trying to comprehend biblical leadership theory is to look for transferable principles clearly identified in Scripture. Several passages help us understand what God means by Christian leadership.

Matthew 20:20–28

The first is found in Matthew 20. The passage surrounds the incident where the mother of James and John came to Jesus and requested that they be able to sit on Jesus's left and right in the kingdom of heaven. The other ten disciples were indignant regarding this request. As a result, Jesus called the disciples together and taught them about leadership.

You know that the *rulers* of the Gentiles *lord* it over them, and their high officials exercise *authority* over them. Not so with you. Instead, whoever wants to become great among you must be your *servant*, and whoever wants to be *first* must be your *slave*—just as the Son of Man did not come to be served, but to *serve*, and to give his life as a ransom for many.

Matthew 20:25–28, italics added

I have italicized the key words in this teaching. The first is "rulers." The Greek word is *archon*, which is translated in various ways but simply means leader. Jesus is addressing the issue of leadership and comparing how leaders in the world act and behave compared with those who serve the church.

The second key word is "lord." This refers to the wrong type of leadership used by those in the world. It implies the use of power, control, and manipulation primarily for the benefit of the leader. Some translations say "to lord it over" or "subdue." There is a definite implication of leading by force.

The next word is "authority." The Greek word is *katakyrieuo*, used only four times in the New Testament. "Exercise authority" is a weak translation of the actual meaning of this word, which more accurately refers to bringing someone under your power, to subdue, to master, to hold in subjection, to be master of, or to exercise lordship over. All of these meanings suggest the abuse of a leadership role. The Greek word used for "great" in referring to those in the kingdom of God who want to lead is the same word used for "high officials" when referring to the secular leaders. Thus, we are to conclude that it is not the issue of leadership that Jesus is questioning but how leadership is exercised.

The word rendered "servant" in the New International Version is *diakonos* in the Greek. This word is used many times in the New Testament and is most often translated "minister." Thus, the word refers to someone who is ministering to another, someone who is serving the needs of others, not just looking out for themselves at the expense of others.

The word "first" is the Greek word *protos*, also used many times in the New Testament, and refers to someone who is first in influence, honor, or authority. Thus, again, Jesus is affirming the concept of leadership, even among Christians.

The word "slave" is the Greek word *doulos*, normally translated as "servant," and means one who serves others or one who is devoted to others.

The word "serve" is *diakoneo* and is the verb form of "servant."

1 Peter 5:1–4

First Peter 5:1–4 is a series of instructions given by the apostle Peter to those who were serving as elders or leaders in the churches.

> To the elders among you, I appeal as a fellow elder, a witness of Christ's sufferings and one who also will share in the glory to be revealed: *Be shepherds of* God's flock that is under your care, *serving*

as overseers—not because you must, but because you are *willing*,
as God wants you to be; not greedy for money, but eager to serve;
not *lording it over those entrusted* to you, but being *examples* to
the flock.

1 Peter 5:1–3, italics added

Again I have italicized some of the key words. The word translated
"be shepherds of" in the NIV is *poimaino*, a verb that means to feed,
tend a flock, nourish, watch over, or lead. However, a particularly interesting use of the word is in the book of Revelation. It is first used
in 2:26–27: "To him who overcomes and does my will to the end, I will
give authority over the nations— 'He will rule them with an iron scep-
ter; he will dash them to pieces like pottery'—just as I have received
authority from my Father." Here the word is used for one who rules
with a significant authority. The same uses are found in 12:5 and 19:15,
where the common English translation is to "rule."

"Serving as overseers" in the Greek is from *episkopeo*. The noun
form of this word is often translated "bishop" in the New Testament.
It refers to one who has oversight and responsibility for the care of
others. From this passage as well as Acts 20:17–35, we can see that
the terms "elders," "overseers," "bishops," "shepherds," and "pastors"
are basically interchangeable. These were the leaders of the first-
century church along with the apostles. The instructions given to them
as well as the list of qualifications given in 1 Timothy and Titus give
us great clues into what was expected of leaders in the early church.
Interestingly, in Timothy and Titus the focus is on the character of
the leader.

The word translated "willing" is important because it implies that
the leaders want to lead.

The Greek verb for "lording it over" is the same word used in the
Matthew passage referring to the wrong type of leadership used by
those in the world.

"Those entrusted" is a very interesting word in the Greek. The word
is *kleros*, meaning what is obtained by lot or what is given by God.
The implication is that God entrusts others to leaders. He sovereignly
places them with leaders, and the good leader is expected to be a good
"steward" or "manager" of that which is entrusted to him.

Finally the word translated "examples" is *typos*, which refers to an
example to be imitated or that is worthy of imitation. In other words, a
good leader is one who is a model for others. By observing the character
and behavior of a good leader, others can learn how to lead.

Hebrews 13:7, 17

In Hebrews 13 the writer is giving his final instructions to his readers:

> Remember your *leaders*, who spoke the word of God to you. Consider the outcome of their way of life and *imitate* their faith. . . . *Obey* your leaders and *submit* to their authority. They keep watch over you as men who must give an *account*. Obey them so that their work will be a joy, not a burden, for that would be of no advantage to you.
>
> Hebrews 13:7, 17, italics added

In the NIV the term "leaders" is used, which in the Greek is from the verb *hegeomai*, which is often translated "to rule over." Other meanings of the word are to go before, command, or have authority over. So once again leadership is recognized as a valuable and necessary part of church life.

The word "imitate" is *mimeomai*, which is where we get the term "mimic." Asking the followers to imitate their leaders implies that the leaders were good examples of the character and behavior expected of them.

"Obey" is *peitho*. Although "obey" is one translation of the word, the more common translation is "be persuaded." Other meanings include to listen, yield to, comply with, trust, and have confidence in. The implication is that the leaders are worthy of the followers' trust and confidence.

The word translated "submit" in the NIV is the Greek word *hypeiko*, which might more accurately be translated "yield." In other words, this is a voluntary act on the part of the followers who are asked to yield to the authority and wisdom of the leaders.

The word translated "account" in the NIV is *logos*, more commonly translated "word." The implication is that leaders are held accountable to give an explanation, a reckoning of what they have done with that which has been entrusted to them. Knowing that leaders are in fact being held accountable by God for how they lead should give followers an added sense of security.

Based on these passages we can make the following conclusions about Christian leaders from the perspective of Scripture:

- They are people who have willingly accepted the opportunity and responsibility God has given them to lead.

- They lead on God's behalf using his spiritual power rather than simply acting on their own self interests. They are dependent on God rather than themselves.
- They have God-given authority and oversight responsibility.
- They are entrusted by God with people who follow them.
- They will give an account of their leadership to God.
- They take their leadership responsibilities seriously and lead with eagerness.
- By the very nature of their responsibilities, they are expected to lead, to go before, to stand before.
- They use their authority to minister or serve the true needs of the followers. Their authority does not come through an "office" or title, and it does not come through rules, regulations, and/or legalistic power.
- They lead by example. They are of such noble character and exemplary leadership that others can imitate them and learn how to become leaders themselves.
- They are not abusive or dictatorial.
- They sacrifice themselves for the good of those they shepherd.
- They protect the flock from outside dangers and internal turmoil.
- Probably most importantly, biblical leadership focuses on character development as foundational to Christian leadership.

Differences between Secular and Biblical Leadership Theory

As you have probably noticed by now, there is a great deal of overlap between secular and biblical leadership theory. Look at the diagram below, which I think demonstrates the major differences between the two.

	Secular Leadership Theory	Biblical Leadership Theory
Primary Focus	Leadership Behavior	Leadership Character
Secondary Focus	Leadership Character	Leadership Behavior

As you can see, both secular and biblical leadership theory include aspects of both leadership behavior and leadership character. The difference is in emphasis. Secular leadership theory does not ignore the issue of character, but most of the focus is on what leaders do—their behavior. Biblical leadership theory does not ignore the issue of behavior, but most of the focus is on the character of leaders, with the clear implication that proper character results in genuine spiritual authority.

For more about this difference, see Paul's descriptions of the qualifications for elders in 1 Timothy 3:1–7 and Titus 5:1–9 and for deacons in 1 Timothy 3:8–13 as well as Peter's description of the qualifications for elders in 1 Peter 5:1–11.

It is clear from these passages that while some behavioral issues are mentioned, the biblical emphasis is on character issues. The biblical view is that proper leadership behavior should flow out of proper leadership character. This is why so much of God's training process for Christian leaders focuses on character development.

> Character is who you are, not just what you do. Leaders are social artists. Their influence transcends what they do and how they solve problems. Their actions and attitudes influence and model leadership.[17]
>
> Alan Nelson and Stan Toler

Summary

Christian leadership is the process of guiding a group of people in a godly way so that they accomplish God's purposes for themselves and at the same time impact the world they live in for Jesus Christ.

Guiding—This emphasizes the role of the Christian leader as one who goes in front, one who initiates, one who is proactive, one who serves rather than one who is autocratic. Guiding does not carry the negative baggage that is characteristic of other terms used for leadership, such as lead, govern, rule, and so on.

Group of people—There is no such thing as a Christian leader without followers. Christian leaders are entrusted with a specific group of people.

In a godly way—The guiding must be done within the context of godly Christian character. The foundation for proper leadership is character that represents the person and teachings of Jesus Christ. As true leaders they ask God, wait, reflect on, discern, check out, and act.

Accomplish—With effective leadership there is a genuine purpose and direction, there is accountability, there is stewardship, and there is an expectation of achievement.

God's purposes for themselves—God has a dual purpose in ministry. While people are accomplishing things for God, they also are continually being changed more and more into the likeness of Jesus Christ. This includes the development of character as well as the discovery of one's specific place and function in the body of Christ. Christian leaders must understand that they are not just trying to accomplish something for God but also are responsible for "raising up" and "equipping" those who are going to do the ministry.

Impact the world they live in for Jesus Christ—This emphasizes the fulfillment of the unique assignments God has given to his people here on Earth. We are here to make a difference. We are here to present Christ to the world through our actions and behaviors. Effective Christian leaders understand their role and responsibilities, and through the groups they lead and equip, they accomplish God's purposes in this world.

Questions for Reflection

1. Do you believe leaders are born or made? Why?
2. With which principles of secular leadership theory do you agree or disagree? Why?
3. With which principles of biblical leadership theory do you agree or disagree? Why?
4. Which parts of the definition given at the end of the chapter for Christian leadership resonate with what you believe? Why? Which do not resonate with your own beliefs? Why not?

5

GOD'S TRAINING PROCESS FOR CHRISTIAN LEADERS

- **■ SCRIPTURAL LEADERSHIP PRINCIPLES**
- **■ OVERVIEW OF GOD'S TRAINING PROCESS FOR LEADERS**
- **■ COMMON PHASES IN GOD'S TRAINING PROCESS**
- **■ SUMMARY**

Effective spiritual ministry flows out of being, and God is concerned with our being. He is forming it. The patterns and processes He uses to shape us are worthwhile subjects for leadership study. Those who study patterns and processes, and use insights from them in life and ministry, will be better prepared leaders.[1]

J. Robert Clinton

God's conditions must be complied with in secret before He will
honor a man in public.[2]

J. Oswald Sanders

"For I know the plans I have for you," declares the LORD, "plans
to prosper you and not to harm you, plans to give you hope and a
future."

Jeremiah 29:11

What is man that you make so much of him, that you give him so
much attention, that you examine him every morning and test him
every moment?

Job 7:17–18

The steps of the godly are directed by the Lord. He delights in every
detail of their lives.

Psalm 37:23 NLT

The Lord will work out his plans for my life.

Psalm 138:8 NLT

R alph knew that ministry was difficult and required substantial
sacrifice on his part, but after ten years of total effort, the fruit of
his ministry seemed very minimal. He began to wonder if he was the
source of the problems, if maybe he wasn't cut out for the ministry, if
maybe what he had felt as a call to ministry was just his own idea. It
was a very discouraging time for Ralph and unfortunately the leadership team in the church was not a great deal of help. In fact, several of
the key leaders were passively resisting every new thing Ralph tried
to bring to the church. Ralph decided if he was really going to make a
difference, he needed to get a clearer perspective on his ministry and
increase his leadership skills.

As the result of a five-year process of self-examination, classes at a
practically focused seminary, and working with a very influential mentor in his area, Ralph emerged as a very confident and focused leader.
Slowly but surely the lessons he learned began to pay off. He began
to see the fruit he had wanted to see many years earlier. The next
ten years became the most fruitful of his entire career. He could look
back and see where God had taken him and why, and he was thankful
for learning the lessons that had allowed him to be an effective and
influential leader.

I am indebted to the work of Dr. Robert Clinton of Fuller Seminary in the area of Christian leadership development. His book *The Making of a Leader* is foundational for understanding how God trains and equips leaders. The material in this chapter is based in part on Clinton's work but is significantly modified, adapted, and expanded based on my teaching and training experience with pastors and ministry leaders.

Scriptural Leadership Principles

1. **God develops a leader over a lifetime. His top priority is to conform leaders to the image of Christ so that they can minister in genuine spiritual authority. Fruitfulness flows out of being. Ministry flows from character. That is why character must be developed first. Spiritual authority is a by-product of character.**

Such confidence as this is ours through Christ before God. Not that we are competent in ourselves to claim anything for ourselves, but our competence comes from God.

2 Corinthians 3:4–5

For this very reason, make every effort to add to your faith goodness; and to goodness, knowledge; and to knowledge, self-control; and to self-control, perseverance; and to perseverance, godliness; and to godliness, brotherly kindness; and to brotherly kindness, love. For if you possess these qualities in increasing measure, they will keep you from being ineffective and unproductive in your knowledge of our Lord Jesus Christ.

2 Peter 1:5–8

I am the true vine, and my Father is the gardener. He cuts off every branch in me that bears no fruit, while every branch that does bear fruit he prunes so that it will be even more fruitful. You are already clean because of the word I have spoken to you. Remain in me, and I will remain in you. No branch can bear fruit by itself; it must remain in the vine. Neither can you bear fruit unless you remain in me. I am the vine; you are the branches. If a man remains

in me and I in him, he will bear much fruit; apart from me you can
do nothing.

John 15:1–5

It is normal for us to focus more on what we do than on who we
are, but God sees things in the reverse order. He works first on our
character because he knows that fruitful ministry follows solid character. We are anxious to get on with God's work and often cannot
understand all the delays along the way. But God's timing is best.
A study of God's great men and women in the Bible demonstrates
a significant amount of time spent on character development. The
ones who learned well, finished well. Those who did not faltered
along the way.

**2. Leadership is something that is entrusted to faithful
men and women. Leaders are expected to prove worthy of
this trust.**

Brothers, think of what you were when you were called. Not many of
you were wise by human standards; not many were influential; not
many were of noble birth. But God chose the foolish things of the
world to shame the wise; God chose the weak things of the world to
shame the strong. He chose the lowly things of this world and the
despised things—and the things that are not—to nullify the things
that are, so that no one may boast before him.

1 Corinthians 1:26–29

We, however, will not boast beyond proper limits, but will confine
our boasting to the field God has assigned to us, a field that reaches
even to you. . . . But, "Let him who boasts boast in the Lord." For it
is not the one who commends himself who is approved, but the one
whom the Lord commends.

2 Corinthians 10:13, 17–18

Often when we accept leadership opportunities, we fail to understand the real responsibility that goes along with the opportunity. The
whole concept of stewardship is based on the idea that we have been
given something that is very special, and we are expected to treat it
that way. The good and faithful servant is the one who recognizes
that God has entrusted him with every ministry opportunity, and he

serves accordingly. Ministry opportunities are not to be treated lightly or frivolously, regardless of whether the assignment is large or small, visible or behind the scenes.

3. **Ministry is not something we own or control. We are simply stewards of what God chooses to entrust to us. To the degree that we are faithful and obedient, our sphere of influence is increased or decreased. Growth in personal development results in a higher level of ministry opportunity, which in turn brings out a need for increased personal development.**

Now it is required that those who have been given a trust must prove faithful.

1 Corinthians 4:2

Whoever can be trusted with very little can also be trusted with much, and whoever is dishonest with very little will also be dishonest with much. So if you have not been trustworthy in handling worldly wealth, who will trust you with true riches?

Luke 16:10–11

As we learned from the parable of the talents, we are expected to do something significant with what God has given to us. It's not enough to just hold on to what he has given us. As we effectively fulfill our assignment, we are led to more challenging assignments. Our sphere of influence often grows with increased responsibility. However, we usually discover it requires an even greater dependence on God and his provision. Increased opportunity also provides an increased challenge to our character, which is also part of God's personal development plan for us.

4. **The primary difference between those who continue in ministry and eventually flourish versus those who drop out along the way is perseverance (or patience).**

Perseverance must finish its work so that you may be mature and complete, not lacking anything.

James 1:4

Therefore, since we are surrounded by such a great cloud of witnesses, let us throw off everything that hinders and the sin that so easily entangles, and let us run with perseverance the race marked out for us. Let us fix our eyes on Jesus, the author and perfecter of our faith, who for the joy set before him endured the cross, scorning its shame, and sat down at the right hand of the throne of God. Consider him who endured such opposition from sinful men, so that you will not grow weary and lose heart.

Hebrews 12:1–3

You need to persevere so that when you have done the will of God, you will receive what he has promised.

Hebrews 10:35

The New Testament uses the word for patience or perseverance often. We begin to see a pattern as we read the different biblical passages. The result of God's processing in our lives is meant to be the development of perseverance, which is critical to our Christian walk. We are not expected to enjoy all the testing and trials, but we are expected to enjoy the spiritual fruit that we develop in our lives as the result of those events. Perseverance is the one common denominator of leaders who finish well. Lack of perseverance is the most common denominator of those who fail in the parable of the soils, found in Matthew 13:3–23, Mark 4:3–20, and Luke 8:5–15. Notice, however, in Luke's version that Jesus gives the reason for the success of the farmer with the good soil—the soil that produced a hundred times what was sown. He sums it up in one word: "perserverance."

5. Mature character comes through difficult testing. Many leaders go through such tests without realizing the benefit.

But he said to me, "My grace is sufficient for you, for my power is made perfect in weakness." Therefore I will boast all the more gladly about my weaknesses, so that Christ's power may rest on me. That is why, for Christ's sake, I delight in weaknesses, in insults, in hardships, in persecutions, in difficulties. For when I am weak, then I am strong.

2 Corinthians 12:9–10

Blessed is the man who perseveres under trial, because when he has stood the test, he will receive the crown of life that God has promised to those who love him.

James 1:12

The suffering you sent was good for me, for it taught me to pay attention to your principles.

Psalm 119:71 NLT

We spend an inordinate amount of time figuring out creative ways to avoid pain at all cost. But all pain is not bad. In fact, in many instances pain leads to growth. Most of us can see this in retrospect, but it is much more difficult to see it when we are in the midst of pain. When we look in the rearview mirror of our lives, we can see that some of the most difficult periods produced the greatest development in our character. Sometimes even the pain we had to suffer unjustly from the behavior of others can be turned into something beneficial. Our personal attitude has a lot to do with how well we process negative events in our lives. If we simply become victims, we seldom learn. But if we strive to see God in the midst of every situation, we are often surprised at the lessons we learn.

6. Being a "servant-leader" means you are willing to do both, not just one or the other.

Be shepherds of God's flock that is under your care, serving as overseers—not because you must, but because you are willing, as God wants you to be; not greedy for money, but eager to serve; not lording it over those entrusted to you, but being examples to the flock.

1 Peter 5:2–3

I am the good shepherd. The good shepherd lays down his life for the sheep. The hired hand is not the shepherd who owns the sheep. So when he sees the wolf coming, he abandons the sheep and runs away. Then the wolf attacks the flock and scatters it. The man runs away because he is a hired hand and cares nothing for the sheep.

John 10:11–13

As we discussed in a previous chapter, many Christian leaders work extremely hard at being servants but do not spend the same amount of time and energy in becoming leaders. Thus, they are incomplete and usually ineffective servant-leaders. You cannot be a leader unless you are willing to be a servant first. Jesus clearly taught this. But being an effective servant does not automatically lead to effective leadership. We will need to employ other characteristics and behaviors to provide the right kind of leadership. Jesus is a wonderful example of both. While truly a servant in every way, he provided the quality of leadership that allowed the disciples he trained to turn the world upside down.

7. To be a leader means that you are willing to be focused, intentional, and proactive.

As we have discussed throughout this book, leadership has many different traits and characteristics. But three things are absolutely essential for effective leadership.

Focused. Everybody has an agenda for us; however, it may not be God's agenda. And unless we are able to focus, we will go aimlessly through life, guided only by other people's agendas and the circumstances of life. Leaders are able to filter all of these things and focus their energies on the things that are truly important. They are able to discern the difference between what is good and what is best. As Paul wrote to the Corinthians, "Do you not know that in a race all the runners run, but only one gets the prize? Run in such a way as to get the prize. Everyone who competes in the games goes into strict training. They do it to get a crown that will not last; but we do it to get a crown that will last forever. Therefore I do not run like a man running aimlessly; I do not fight like a man beating the air. No, I beat my body and make it my slave so that after I have preached to others, I myself will not be disqualified for the prize" (1 Cor. 9:24–27).

Intentional. Intentionality is another critical characteristic of effective leaders. Their clarity of focus leads them to specific action steps to accomplish their purposes. They take a rifle approach to life rather than a shotgun approach. They drive the agenda as they discern God's will for their lives. They aggressively pursue what they have purposed for themselves.

Proactive. Most people, even leaders, if they examined their lives thoroughly, would find that they spend more time reacting to things than initiating. But effective leaders are exactly the opposite. While aware of their circumstances, they don't wait for something to happen before they begin to move. They don't spend all their time fighting fires; they spend more time figuring out ways to prevent fires or in some cases starting fires purposely. Proverbs 13:16 says, "A wise man thinks ahead; a fool doesn't" (TLB).

Overview of God's Training Process for Leaders

The LORD will fulfill his purpose for me.

Psalm 138:8

For physical training is of some value, but godliness has value for all things, holding promise for both the present life and the life to come.

1 Timothy 4:8

In looking at the training process God used with leaders in the Old and New Testaments and comparing it with the training process of Christian leaders throughout history, it is obvious that there are some common stages or phases that virtually all leaders go through.

In the early stages "success" may or may not occur. It is possible for leaders to be successful in ministry and still fail in character development, thereby delaying or destroying further ministry opportunity. The reason they may initially succeed is solely because of the spiritual gifts they have received from God. Spiritual gifts operate regardless of spiritual maturity.

As potential leaders move into ministry, God develops their leadership abilities by taking them through approximately five stages:

- God challenges the leaders into ministry.
- God develops skills in the leaders to enhance their effectiveness.
- God enables the leaders to relate to people in ways that will motivate, influence, and inspire.
- God teaches the leaders how to accomplish his objectives.
- God enables the leaders to see spiritual principles that govern ministry and are reproducible in all ministry settings.

Throughout a leader's life God works to deepen character as well as to develop ministry skills. Mature leaders learn that they must constantly depend on God rather than themselves by God's providential design. Leaders face unexpected situations involving sickness, crises, and conflict. Although few recognize these times as a necessary part of their training for effective ministry, most can look back and see God's hand in their development.

God does not stop working on character after moving someone into leadership. God continues to form character throughout the ministry of a leader. Qualities such as love, compassion, empathy, and discernment are deepened. Such qualities differentiate between a successful leader and a mature successful leader. This deepening of character as well as the leader's relationship with God overflows into ministry itself. A leader who has matured exercises ministry with a new level of spiritual authority. God's training process for leaders usually results in one of four outcomes.

Some leaders drop out. There are many reasons why leaders choose to drop out of God's training process; however, the two most common are as follows:

- Some leaders begin to develop a modern form of legalism where they try to reduce God and his principles to oversimplistic formulas and rules. When these fail, they become discouraged and drop out.
- Some leaders begin to depend increasingly on experiences to maintain their faith. They go from one mountaintop experience to another and try to sustain themselves in between. When this strategy fails, they become discouraged and drop out.

Some leaders plateau at some level of ministry competency and show relatively little growth in ministry or spiritual development. Leaders often reach a point in the later phases where their development seems to be stalled. Leaders have a tendency to cease developing once they have some initial skills and ministry experience. Often they do not notice that they are not growing, particularly in spiritual formation. God often breaks into the leader's life at this point.

When a leader has potential for leadership that is not yet developed, God will challenge that leader to take steps to develop and use that capacity for his purposes. The normal pattern for when a leader plateaus is as follows:

1. God initiates growth processes or tests to gain the attention of the leader.
2. The leader is forced to do serious reflection about ministry, life, and his or her personal relationship with God.
3. The leader does a serious evaluation of who he or she is and what he or she wants to be.
4. The leader experiences a renewed determination to know God more deeply.

5. God blesses the renewed commitment and determination and therefore deepens the relationship between himself and the leader.

If a leader refuses to see the hand of God during this time but instead blames circumstances or people, this positive pattern may not develop, and the result will be a leadership casualty.

Some leaders are disciplined in ministry or totally removed from it. While God is patient and long-suffering, church history clearly shows there is a limit. At some point God will expose the character flaws of the leader, and, depending on the seriousness of those flaws, the leader will suffer from God's discipline. King Saul in the Old Testament is a good example of such a leader.

Some leaders reflect on the meaning of ministry and God's purposes in it and make adjustments as necessary. They remain active learners in God's never-ending training process. The gradual shift for this last group is from simple competency in doing ministry tasks to effectiveness flowing from being a growing disciple of Jesus Christ. These leaders begin to see and understand God's purposes in their ministries. They are compelled not only to deepen their own Christian walk but to share in Christ's passion for ministry.

Those who stay in ministry over the long haul are the exceptions. They are the ones who have responded correctly to God's training process and have learned how to become genuine leaders with spiritual authority.

If you study the maturing process of a great number of spiritual giants from past years, you would conclude that it took them a significant number of years to advance to a mature ministry level. This is evidenced when the leader ceases trying to work for God and instead allows God to do his work through them.

Common Phases in God's Training Process

The common phases of development for emerging leaders are shown below. In the first three phases the emphasis is on proper character development and training, not on production or results. God wants to teach the emerging leader that ministry flows out of being a faithful and righteous person.

This upward development pattern continues throughout a leader's life. It is a spiral of growth in being and doing. In each cycle there is an increased depth in experiencing and knowing God as well as in effective service for God. If the leader does not drop out or plateau along the way, the final result is a melding of being and doing.

Phase 1—Foundations

Beginning at birth God providentially works through the leader's family, environment, and circumstances to prepare a leader even before he or she knows or realizes what God is doing.

Phase 2—Character Development

The crucible for silver and the furnace for gold, but the LORD tests the heart.

Proverbs 17:3

This is where leaders get to know God personally, and the process begins when leaders make a personal commitment to Jesus Christ and choose to be a Christ follower (a Christian). They receive spiritual gifts that help them prepare for specific ministry callings.

In this phase leadership potential is identified, and God uses testing experiences primarily to develop character. If you look at the requirements listed in 1 Timothy 3:2–7, it is striking that of the fourteen qualities listed, eleven are issues of character.

The growing leader invariably gets involved in some form of ministry. Because churches are desperate for volunteers and particularly lay leaders, the potential leader will likely be recognized and recruited early.

Unfortunately, most churches do not have well-designed training processes for these emerging leaders, so they have to learn on the job with little input from others. Ministry opportunities may or may not be in alignment with their spiritual gifts and may involve little leadership opportunity.

Phase 3—Ministry Development

In this phase the emphasis is on two main areas:

- Learning basic ministry skills and learning how to use one's spiritual gifts.

- Learning how the church operates and learning the complexities of relationships that exist in a church environment.

Potential leaders may or may not obtain formal training to improve their ministry skills. They may simply develop them by observation, practice, mentoring, or discipling. Character issues are still being developed and tested, but the emphasis is now on ministry preparation.

Phase 4—Advanced Ministry Training

In this phase leaders normally move into some kind of official leadership position. They are able to develop their ministry and relationship skills further while in this leadership position.

Every aspect of the leader's character will continue to be tested as will his or her ministry skills. Fruitfulness (success) may or may not take place. It depends on the degree to which the leader has the necessary character qualities and has developed the necessary ministry skills. In addition, the ministry context may determine to a great degree the level of success.

Phase 5—Mature Ministry (Fruitfulness)

Leaders who reach this stage have the character qualities and ministry skills necessary for fruitful ministry. They know themselves well and therefore find ministry opportunities where they are likely to succeed. The leaders now know their own strengths and weaknesses and position themselves where those strengths are multiplied and the weaknesses modified. Ministry context is now aligned with the personality and values of the leader. In this phase the leader's ministry potential is fully realized.

Leaders can still make major failures in this phase if they fail character tests, do not properly use their ministry skills, or put themselves into ministry contexts where they cannot succeed.

Phase 6—Afterglow

Unfortunately, only a few reach this phase. It is the culmination of a lifetime of personal growth and ministry. The leader is now recognized by others and is able to influence a very broad spectrum geographically or denominationally. Many emerging leaders will seek such a leader out because of the wisdom he or she has acquired over the years. Paul was in this phase when in his second letter to Timothy he wrote, "I have fought the good fight, I have finished the race, I have kept the faith. Now there is in store for me the crown of righteousness, which the Lord, the righteous Judge, will award to me on that day—and not only to me, but also to all who have longed for his appearing" (2 Tim. 4:7–8).

Example of God's Training Process: Joseph (Genesis 37–50)

And he sent a man before them—Joseph, sold as a slave. They bruised his feet with shackles, his neck was put in irons, till what he foretold came to pass, till the word of the LORD proved him true.

Psalm 105:17–19

The life of Joseph is a wonderful example of how God trains a leader.

PHASE 1—FOUNDATIONS

God was working in Joseph's life from the moment of his conception. He allowed Joseph to become the son of Jacob, who would become the father of the tribes of Israel. Joseph's mother was Rachel, who was Jacob's favorite wife.

PHASE 2—CHARACTER DEVELOPMENT

Until the time came to fulfill his word, the Lord tested Joseph's character.

Psalm 105:19 NLT

When Joseph was only a boy, his father, Jacob, honored him by giving him a special coat. This coat was a symbol of the special love that Jacob had for his son. However, it immediately caused discord and dissension with Joseph's brothers, both because he was younger than them and because their father favored Joseph. This stage of Joseph's life can be compared to the salvation experience in the Christian life and the great sense of favor we have as we begin our walk with God. However, sometimes our family relationships are strained by our new direction in life.

Joseph also antagonized his brothers by bringing a bad report to their father about them. In addition, Joseph received two major dreams that he shared with his brothers and father. Joseph now had lots of zeal and enthusiasm but little spiritual maturity or character. Hence, he was misusing his spiritual gifts.

It is not unusual for God to give us a picture or vision of the future so that we can stay focused and encouraged as we move through the maturing process. However, we often mix up the ends with the means, particularly misunderstanding God's timing. Everything Joseph saw in his dreams would come to pass, but Joseph needed to grow in character through the training and discipline of the Lord.

PHASE 3—MINISTRY DEVELOPMENT

Joseph's brothers became so angry and enraged against their brother that they plotted to kill him. At the age of seventeen Joseph was put in a pit by his brothers to die, but at the last minute they changed their minds and decided to sell him into slavery instead. Joseph was definitely moving into the "things get worse before they get better" phase of his training and a very difficult isolation test. (I'll discuss these tests in greater depth in chapter 6.)

Providentially, Joseph was sold to Potiphar who was the captain of the palace guard of Pharaoh. Joseph submits to Potiphar and eventually is put in charge of everything Potiphar had. Joseph began to demonstrate additional spiritual gifts and was also growing in character. Joseph was being tested and trained by God in many areas of his life.

> The LORD was with Joseph and he prospered, and he lived in the house of his Egyptian master. When his master saw that the LORD was with him and that the LORD gave him success in everything he did, Joseph found favor in his eyes and became his attendant. Potiphar put him in charge of his household, and he entrusted to his care everything he owned. From the time he put him in charge of his household and of all that he owned, the LORD blessed the household of the Egyptian because of Joseph. The blessing of the LORD was on everything Potiphar had, both in the house and in the field. So he left in Joseph's care everything he had; with Joseph in charge, he did not concern himself with anything except the food he ate.
>
> Genesis 39:2–6

Even though Joseph began to succeed in his new position, his character was put to a severe test when Potiphar's wife tried to seduce him.

"Look," [Joseph] told her, "my master trusts me with everything
in his entire household. No one here has more authority than I do!
He has held back nothing from me except you, because you are his
wife. How could I ever do such a wicked thing? It would be a great
sin against God."

Genesis 39:8–9

Even though Joseph passed this integrity test, the result was a
return to prison and another isolation test. Joseph continued to learn
through his experiences. While he did not receive training in the formal
sense, he was constantly developing both his leadership skills as well
as his character.

PHASE 4—ADVANCED MINISTRY TRAINING

Eventually Joseph was put in charge of all the prisoners. He learned
additional skills about leading people in a difficult circumstance. He
successfully passed another authority/submission test as well as an
influence test, as the following passage points out:

> But while Joseph was there in the prison, the LORD was with him;
> he showed him kindness and granted him favor in the eyes of the
> prison warden. So the warden put Joseph in charge of all those held
> in the prison, and he was made responsible for all that was done
> there. The warden paid no attention to anything under Joseph's
> care, because the LORD was with Joseph and gave him success in
> whatever he did.

Genesis 39:20–23

Joseph also passed a spiritual power test when he demonstrated
the gift of interpreting dreams with two of Pharaoh's servants. Notice
that he was able to interpret the dreams as well as acknowledge God
as the source of his gift. The development of his character and spiritual
maturity were clearly evident.

However, the servant who was supposed to remember Joseph and
help him get out of prison failed to do so. Once again Joseph was
tested as he had to decide how he would respond to this betrayal by
Pharaoh's servant. We don't know exactly how he responded, but we
do know he spent over two more years in jail. This was a real faith test.
During this phase of God's training process, every aspect of Joseph's
character was tested as well as his leadership skills.

PHASE 5—MATURE MINISTRY (FRUITFULNESS)

Finally Joseph's opportunity came when Pharaoh had a dream that his magicians could not interpret. Pharaoh's servant remembered Joseph and told Pharaoh about him. Pharaoh summoned Joseph, and Joseph gave a correct interpretation of his dreams. Notice again that Joseph first gave credit to God for his ability to interpret the dream.

> "It is beyond my power to do this," Joseph replied. "But God will tell you what it means and will set you at ease."
>
> Genesis 41:16

Not only was Joseph able to interpret the dream, he knew what to do about it. Pharaoh recognized Joseph's abilities and put him in charge of everything. Finally Joseph put on the clothes of a prince and moved into a palace at thirty years of age.

While in the palace Joseph demonstrated incredible character and wisdom in dealing with a conflict test with his brothers. All of Egypt and Israel began to suffer from famine, and Jacob heard that there was grain available in Egypt. Jacob sent Joseph's brothers to buy some, not knowing that the son he thought was dead was actually in charge of everything in Egypt. While it appeared that Joseph had some fun in tricking his brothers when they did not recognize him, he eventually demonstrated a genuine understanding of forgiveness and the importance of restoring relationships when he reunited with his family. Joseph was able to see the purposes of God in everything that happened to him, and he explained this to his brothers.

> Don't be afraid of me. Am I God, to judge and punish you? As far as I am concerned, God turned into good what you meant for evil. He brought me to the high position I have today so I could save the lives of many people. No, don't be afraid. Indeed, I myself will take care of you and your families.
>
> Genesis 50:19–21

Joseph reached the stage where his character qualities and leadership skills allowed him to have a very fruitful ministry. Joseph's ministry potential was finally realized. This was not only a personal victory for Joseph, but it paved the way for the growth and expansion of the people of Israel. God was working for the good of Israel at the same time he was training his servant Joseph.

Phase 6—Afterglow

The final phase of Joseph's life was eighty years of success and prosperity. He reached the culmination of his personal growth and ministry. He was able to influence the history and direction of the people of Israel.

> Then Joseph said to his brothers, "I am about to die. But God will surely come to your aid and take you up out of this land to the land he promised on oath to Abraham, Isaac and Jacob." And Joseph made the sons of Israel swear an oath and said, "God will surely come to your aid, and then you must carry my bones up from this place."
>
> Genesis 50:24–25

The story of the life of Joseph is the longest and most detailed account of anyone in the book of Genesis. It also serves as a wonderful opportunity to understand God's training process for leaders. Joseph at the end of his life could have spoken words similar to the ones Paul spoke many years later:

> I have fought the good fight, I have finished the race, I have kept the faith. Now there is in store for me the crown of righteousness, which the Lord, the righteous Judge, will award to me on that day—and not only to me, but also to all who have longed for his appearing.
>
> 2 Timothy 4:7–8

We can learn several principles from the life of Joseph.

- Our spiritual gifts can operate independent of spiritual maturity. We might think we are ready to lead yet be without sufficient character development. God must put us through a learning process first.
- God wants us to pass the tests he allows us to face. If we take the time to see the test from God's perspective, we can appropriate his provision for the test.
- We progress by *how* we go through something, not just because we get through it. God will run us through the same test until we learn what we are supposed to learn.
- There is no such thing as leadership without difficult testing and processing.

- Learning to lead means learning to submit, even in difficult circumstances.
- It's a lot easier to see God's purpose and plans in retrospect than it is to understand them while you are in process. Time is an excellent healer and discerner.

Summary

As Christians we often fail to understand God's purposes for what we are going through and therefore miss key learning opportunities that will allow us to grow as Christians. Yet as we have seen in this chapter, God does have a definite training and equipping process for his leaders. His plan is unique to every individual but has some common patterns. He trains us both in character development as well as in ministry skills.

Any learning experience is significantly more valuable if the learner is a willing participant and has a genuine desire to grow. If we resist the training or if we are passive participants, chances are we will miss the key lessons we are supposed to learn. Thus, Christian leaders must approach God's training process with readiness and expectation. It doesn't mean we will personally enjoy every aspect of the training process, but we should attempt to understand God's purpose and seek his wisdom as we grow.

As we partner with God in his growth processes, we accelerate our spiritual growth and develop skills that lead to personal peace and well-being as well as more effective ministry.

> I will instruct you and teach you in the way you should go; I will counsel you and watch over you.
> Psalm 32:8

> But the plans of the LORD stand firm forever, the purposes of his heart through all generations.
> Psalm 33:11

Questions for Reflection

1. Which leadership principle given at the beginning of this chapter is most difficult for you? What are the implications for your personal growth as well as your ministry effectiveness?

2. From the information given in this chapter, which phase of God's training process are you in? Why?

3. Which principles from the life of Joseph do you think you have learned? Which principles do you think you have yet to learn or need to work on in the future? What are the implications for your present ministry assignment?

6

GOD'S GROWTH
PROCESSES

- AUTHORITY/SUBMISSION TESTS
- CONFLICT TESTS
- FAITH TESTS
- INFLUENCE TESTS
- INTEGRITY TESTS
- ISOLATION TESTS
- LEADERSHIP CONFLICT TESTS
- OBEDIENCE TESTS
- PRAYER TESTS
- SPIRITUAL POWER TESTS
- SPIRITUAL WARFARE TESTS
- SUMMARY

Character cannot be developed in ease and quiet. Only through experiences of trial and suffering can the soul be strengthened, vision cleared, ambition inspired and success achieved. . . . The marvelous richness of human experience would lose something of rewarding joy if there were no limitations to overcome. The hilltop hour would not be half so wonderful if there were no dark valleys to traverse.[1]

Helen Keller

No discipline seems pleasant at the time, but painful. Later on, however, it produces a harvest of righteousness and peace for those who have been trained by it.

Hebrews 12:11

It was Hezekiah who blocked the upper outlet of the Gihon spring and channeled the water down to the west side of the City of David. He succeeded in everything he undertook. But when envoys were sent by the rulers of Babylon to ask him about the miraculous sign that had occurred in the land, God left him to test him and to know everything that was in his heart.

2 Chronicles 32:30–31

I tested your faith at Meribah, when you complained that there was no water.

Psalm 81:7 NLT

Until the time came to fulfill his word, the Lord tested Joseph's character.

Psalm 105:19 NLT

God uses providential events, people, and circumstances to develop leaders. It is not always easy to know exactly which test God is using in our growth process. They often do not fit into neat categories. A single test may involve a combination of several different tests. A proper response allows a leader to learn the fundamental lessons God wants to teach. If the leader doesn't learn them, he or she will usually be tested again in the same areas and the length of time of development is increased. A proper response will result in a move toward the next phase of ministry and often will include an expansion of the sphere of influence. God's tests can be barriers or bridges to leadership development depending on the response of the leader. Psalm 119:71 says, "It was good for me to be afflicted so that I might learn your decrees."

The following are some general descriptions of the major tests God uses in the leader's growth process.

Authority/Submission Tests

Jesus called them together and said, "You know that the rulers of the Gentiles lord it over them, and their high officials exercise authority over them. Not so with you. Instead, whoever wants to become great among you must be your servant, and whoever wants to be first must be your slave—just as the Son of Man did not come to be served, but to serve, and to give his life as a ransom for many."

Matthew 20:25–28

For everyone who exalts himself will be humbled, and he who humbles himself will be exalted.

Luke 18:14

The ultimate goal in developing genuine authority and learning proper submission is to help leaders understand that spiritual authority is the real foundation in leadership influence. Authority tests concern how a leader gets along with people: his leaders, his peers, and his subordinates. They refer to positive and negative ministry lessons that teach us about the use of spiritual authority. Authority or submission tests are those instances where a leader learns either positive or negative lessons about relating to other Christians in the course of ministry. Lessons learned through these insights can significantly affect future leadership opportunities.

Types of authority/submission tests include:

1. Submission to authority
2. Understanding authority structures
3. Understanding the importance of submitting to mentors and/or other mature leaders
4. The authenticity or lack of authenticity of various power bases
5. Authority conflict
6. How to exercise authority

There seems to be a somewhat normal pattern or sequence to authority/submission tests.

- The leader experiences or observes a negative use of authority.
- The leader searches and seeks to understand what is legitimate authority.
- The leader develops a desire to model legitimate authority.
- The leader learns insights about spiritual authority.
- The leader experiences an increase of spiritual authority as a source of power.

Scriptural examples include:

1. Cain failed in responding to God (Gen. 4:3–8).
2. Abraham gave a tithe to Melchizedek (Gen. 14:17–20).
3. Jacob submitted to Laban even though Laban was dishonest (Gen. 29:25–31:55).
4. Moses failed in responding to the complaints of people (Num. 11:11–15).
5. Elisha submitted to mentoring by Elijah (1 Kings 19:16–21; 2 Kings 2:1–16).
6. David passed in his confrontation with Goliath (1 Sam. 17:45–47).
7. David passed in his decision not to kill King Saul (1 Sam. 24:4–7; 26:9–11). In 2 Samuel 1:23 we see David's true attitude.
8. Ruth remained loyal to Naomi (Ruth 1:8–18).
9. Timothy and others submitted to mentoring by the apostle Paul.

Conflict Tests

Make every effort to keep the unity of the Spirit through the bond of peace.

Ephesians 4:3

If it is possible, as far as it depends on you, live at peace with everyone.

Romans 12:18

What causes fights and quarrels among you? Don't they come from your desires that battle within you? You want something but don't get it. You kill and covet, but you cannot have what you want. You quarrel and fight. You do not have, because you do not ask God. When you ask, you do not receive, because you ask with wrong motives, that you may spend what you get on your pleasures.

James 4:1–3

When people influence other people, conflict inevitably arises. Conflict tests refer to those situations where a leader learns either positive or negative lessons about what it takes to be a true leader during difficult circumstances. A leader's grasp of these lessons can significantly affect future leadership opportunities. Conflict may come from without (i.e., from those who are not believers) and from within (i.e., from those who are believers). Sometimes the conflict from within is the most difficult to face since a leader has higher expectations for believers.

Ministry conflict, like general conflict, tests a leader's spiritual maturity. What we truly are is revealed in a crisis.

Unfortunately, oftentimes leaders do not experience firm closure to their conflicts. Closure completes an experience. It allows us to learn the necessary lesson as well as put the negative aspects of the conflict behind us. It is important to have closure in conflicts; otherwise it will be hard to learn the necessary lessons. It is bad enough to go through conflict. It is worse to go through conflict and not profit from it.

Types of conflict tests include:

1. Understanding the nature of conflict
2. Learning possible ways to resolve or avoid conflict
3. Learning creative ways to use conflict
4. Understanding how God uses conflict to develop the leader's inner life

Scriptural examples include:

1. Abraham resolved conflict with Lot (Gen. 13:7–11).
2. Issac refused to fight with Abimelech's herdsmen (Gen. 26:12–33).
3. Jacob reconciled with Esau (Genesis 32–33).
4. Simeon and Levi failed as they deceived and killed men of Shechem (Gen. 34:13).
5. Moses passed most of the tests he faced with the rebellious people of Israel (Exodus 14ff.).
6. Moses failed the test at Meribah (Num. 20:1–13).
7. David passed when he fled from Absalom and was cursed by Shimei (2 Sam. 16:5–12).
8. Nehemiah kept focus on rebuilding the wall of Jerusalem while he dealt with conflicts around him (Nehemiah 4–6).
9. The Council of Jerusalem solved the problem between Jewish and Gentile believers (Acts 15).

Faith Tests

Now faith is being sure of what we hope for and certain of what we do not see. This is what the ancients were commended for. . . . And without faith it is impossible to please God, because anyone who comes to him must believe that he exists and that he rewards those who earnestly seek him.

Hebrews 11:1, 6

We live by faith, not by sight.

2 Corinthians 5:7

And what more shall I say? I do not have time to tell about Gideon, Barak, Samson, Jephthah, David, Samuel and the prophets, who through faith conquered kingdoms, administered justice, and gained what was promised; who shut the mouths of lions, quenched the fury of the flames, and escaped the edge of the sword; whose weakness was turned to strength; and who became powerful in battle and routed foreign armies.

Hebrews 11:32–34

God's call to leaders to increase their faith as they carry out ministry is one of the strongest challenges they will face. Faith challenges almost always stretch people beyond their present understanding. Faith tests are not restricted to those who have the spiritual gift of faith. Faith tests are directly linked to effective ministry. Leaders are people with God-given vision, and one of their functions is to inspire followers with that vision and hope. They can't fulfill this function without faith.

Faith tests refer to those instances in ministry where a leader is challenged by God to take steps of faith in ministry and see God reward those steps with divine affirmation and ministry achievement. God's faithfulness increases the leader's capacity to trust him in future ministry.

The normal pattern in faith tests is as follows:

- The leader receives direction from God concerning some future plan.
- The leader realizes that God is challenging him to act on the basis of this direction.
- The leader determines to make leadership decisions based on these firm convictions.

Scriptural examples include:

1. Noah built the ark (Gen. 6:9–22).
2. Abraham failed when he had Ishmael by Hagar (Gen. 16:1–15).
3. Jacob yielded to God (Gen. 28:10–22).
4. Joseph remained confident through negative circumstances and harbored no bitterness toward his brothers (Gen. 50:19–21).
5. Moses decided to leave Pharaoh's palace to help his Jewish brothers and sisters (Heb. 11:24–25).
6. Aaron failed as he led Israel to build a golden calf (Exod. 32:1–6, 21–26).
7. Gideon failed as he resisted the call of God to be a leader and asked for a sign from God (Judges 6:11–24, 36–40).
8. Saul failed as he consulted with a medium (1 Sam. 28:5–8).
9. David passed a test in his encounter with Goliath (1 Sam. 17:32–37).
10. David demonstrated faith in his instructions to Solomon (1 Chron. 28:20).
11. Joshua failed after a defeat at Ai (Josh. 7:6–13).

Influence Tests

Such confidence as this is ours through Christ before God. Not that we are competent in ourselves to claim anything for ourselves, but our competence comes from God. He has made us competent as ministers of a new covenant—not of the letter but of the Spirit; for the letter kills, but the Spirit gives life.

2 Corinthians 3:4–6

My son, preserve sound judgment and discernment, do not let them out of your sight; they will be life for you, an ornament to grace your neck. Then you will go on your way in safety, and your foot will not stumble; when you lie down, you will not be afraid; when you lie down, your sleep will be sweet. Have no fear of sudden disaster or of the ruin that overtakes the wicked, for the LORD will be your confidence and will keep your foot from being snared.

Proverbs 3:21–26

Influence tests refer to those instances where a leader is prompted by God to expand his sphere of influence. The influence test can come through an increase in extensiveness, intensiveness, or scope of influence.

An influence test is normally a step forward in increased responsibility, but leaders should not consciously seek to expand their sphere of influence as if bigger were better. Leaders are to respond to God's challenge to accept varying spheres of influence in order to find God's proper sphere for them.

Scriptural examples include:

1. Esau failed when he sold his birthright (Gen. 25:29–34).
2. Moses resisted the call of God (Exod. 3:7–4:17).
3. Leaders of Israel failed when they chose to listen to negative reports and were banished from the Promised Land (Num. 13:25–14:23; Deut. 1:19–39).
4. Joshua and Caleb demonstrated confidence in God's new assignment when they spied out the Promised Land (Num. 13:25–30).
5. Jeremiah demonstrated confidence in God's new assignment when God challenged him to be his spokesman (Jer. 1:4–10).
6. Esther demonstrated confidence in God's new assignment when she was challenged to go to the king to save her people, the Jews (Esther 4:7–17).
7. Paul and Barnabas demonstrated confidence in God's new assignment when they were sent out by the church at Antioch on their missionary journeys (Acts 13ff.).

Integrity Tests

Let your "Yes" be yes, and your "No," no, or you will be condemned.

James 5:12

When I planned this, did I do it lightly? Or do I make my plans in a worldly manner so that in the same breath I say, "Yes, yes" and "No, no"? But as surely as God is faithful, our message to you is not "Yes" and "No." For the Son of God, Jesus Christ, who was preached among you by me and Silas and Timothy, was not "Yes" and "No," but in him it has always been "Yes."

2 Corinthians 1:17–19

Integrity is the heart of character. Integrity tests show whether or not the leader is genuine and has credibility. An emerging leader becomes aware of the importance of integrity through these tests. God uses them to evaluate intentions and thereby shape character. There are three parts to an integrity check:

- The leader is challenged to be consistent with his or her inner convictions.
- The leader responds to the challenge rightly (or wrongly).
- The leader experiences expansion (or shrinking) of ministry.

Types of integrity tests include tests of:

1. Values (which determine convictions)
2. Temptation (which tests conviction)
3. Conflict (which tests faith)
4. Persecution (which tests steadfastness)
5. Loyalty (which tests allegiance)
6. Restitution (which tests honesty)

Scriptural examples include:

1. Adam failed in his response to God (Gen. 3:11–12).
2. Abraham failed when he asked Sarah to lie (Gen. 12:11–13).
3. Abraham failed when he asked Sarah to lie again (Gen. 20:2).
4. Issac failed when he lied about Rebekah (Gen. 26:7).
5. Jacob and Rebekah failed when they deceived Issac (Gen. 27:1–40).
6. Joseph resisted Potiphar's wife (Gen. 39:7–18).
7. Joshua challenged the people of Israel to put total trust in God (Josh. 24:15).
8. Eli failed when he refused to discipline his sons (1 Sam. 2:12–35).
9. Saul failed a test with the Amelikites (1 Sam. 15:3, 8–23).
10. David mourned when his men killed Saul's military leader and refused to let his men kill others (2 Sam. 3:26–39).
11. David failed a test with Bathsheba and Uriah (2 Samuel 11) but passed a test with repentance when confronted by Nathan (2 Sam. 12:1–25).

12. David demonstrated integrity when he bought land for an altar (2 Sam. 24:21–24).
13. Gehazi failed a test when he secretly tried to get money from Naaman (2 Kings 5:1–27).
14. Daniel chose not to eat food from the king's table (Dan. 1:8–16).
15. Amaziah refused help of foreign troops and lost money he had spent but followed the prophet's instructions (2 Chron. 25:7–10).
16. Amaziah failed when he worshipped false gods (2 Chron. 25:14–16).
17. Shadrach, Meshach, and Abednego refused to worship the king's gold statue (Dan. 3:13–18).
18. Peter and Barnabas failed when they gave in to Jewish Christians (Gal. 2:11ff.).

Isolation Tests

Be still, and know that I am God.

Psalm 46:9

One way that God forces a leader into reflective evaluation and into a deepening of character involves isolation. It is one of the most effective means for maturing a leader. Sometimes in a leader's lifetime, the leader may be set aside from normal ministry. Causes may include crises, disciplinary action, providential circumstances (such as war, oppressive government action, illness), or the leader's own choice. The determining factor in whether leaders will pass this test is whether or not they recognize that the isolation is God's work and that it is a call to a deeper relationship and experience of God.

Isolation tests are those where a leader is separated from normal ministry involvement, usually for an extended time and experiences new growth in his relationship to God. Isolation is often used by God to teach important leadership lessons that could not be learned while experiencing the pressures of normal ministry context.

Scriptural examples include:

1. Moses in his forty years in the desert (Exod. 2:13–25).
2. Joshua's forty years in the desert.
3. Elijah in the cave (1 Kings 19:1–18).

4. David fleeing from Saul (1 Samuel 21–2 Samuel 2).

5. Job dealt with loss of family, wealth, and health (book of Job).

6. Paul in Arabia (Gal. 1:17–18).

Leadership Conflict Tests

Even my close friend, whom I trusted, he who shared my bread, has lifted up his heel against me.

Psalm 41:9

If an enemy were insulting me, I could endure it; if a foe were raising himself against me, I could hide from him. But it is you, a man like myself, my companion, my close friend, with whom I once enjoyed sweet fellowship as we walked with the throng at the house of God.

Psalm 55:12–14

Leadership conflict tests are a special case of ministry conflict. A leader experiencing leadership conflict learns to submit to God in a deeper way. These tests refer to the negative reactions of other leaders within the group to a course of action taken by a leader.

There is a somewhat common pattern to leadership conflict tests.

- The leader gets a vision (direction) from God.
- The followers are convinced of the direction.
- The group moves in the direction given.
- The group experiences persecution, hard times, or attacks from Satan. Spiritual warfare is common.
- There is a conflict or rebellion from the group.
- The leader is driven to God to seek affirmation.
- God reveals himself: who he is and what he intends to do. He makes it clear that he will deliver.
- God vindicates the leader.

A leader's success brings its own set of problems. All leaders need to be aware of this and persevere through the trials associated with effective ministry. God may have several purposes for these tests, including the development of inner-life maturity.

Leadership conflict tests are a form of integrity testing in which both the leader and the followers' motivations are tested. Followers need to realize that submitting to spiritual authority involves obeying God by being loyal to the leader who is following God's direction. Loyalty is not tested until difficult times come. God can use difficult times to set the stage for deliverance that can come only from him. He can then deliver, receive glory, and lay foundations for future work.

Scriptural examples include:

1. Moses underwent constant criticism from the people of Israel (book of Exodus).
2. Moses was attacked by Miriam and Aaron (Num. 12:1–16).
3. Nehemiah encountered resistance when rebuilding the walls around Jerusalem (Nehemiah 4–6).
4. David's key men revolted against him at Ziklag (1 Sam. 30:6).
5. David had to flee from Absalom (2 Sam. 15:1–12).
6. Jeroboam rebelled against Solomon (1 Kings 11:26–40).
7. Judas betrayed Jesus (Matt. 26:14–16; Luke 22:3–6; John 13:21–30).
8. Many of those around Paul deserted him (2 Tim. 4:6–17).

Obedience Tests

And this is love: that we walk in obedience to his commands.

2 John 6

But Samuel replied: "Does the LORD delight in burnt offerings and sacrifices as much as in obeying the voice of the LORD? To obey is better than sacrifice, and to heed is better than the fat of rams. For rebellion is like the sin of divination, and arrogance like the evil of idolatry."

1 Samuel 15:22

A leader must have the ability to receive truth from God and obey it. The right to influence comes from the ability to clarify God's truth to others. Godly leaders display love for truth. They study the written Word to feed their own souls as well as to help others. They learn to listen to and hear God's spoken truth. God teaches a leader to appreciate truth, cultivate habits for the intake of truth, and respond in obedience to truth, so he or she may be quick to discern God's truth in everyday life.

An obedience test measures a leader's ability to understand or receive God's Word personally and then allow God to work it out in his or her life. When successfully passed, an obedience test will lead to more truth. Truth will confirm the emerging leader's capacity to lead, which will yield an increased spiritual authority as perceived by followers. It is one thing to obey when it seems logical and necessary, but it is quite another when the obedience calls for something that doesn't make sense. Obedience doesn't always hinge on understanding.

Examples of obedience tests include:

1. Learning about possessions and giving
2. Learning to put God first in the choice of a mate
3. Learning to be used by God in ministry
4. Learning to trust a God-given truth
5. Learning to forgive
6. Learning to confess error
7. Learning to right a wrong
8. Learning to have inner convictions
9. Learning to solve problems
10. Learning to clarify guidance

Leaders are responsible for influencing specific groups of people to obey God. They will not achieve this unless they themselves know how to obey.

Scriptural examples include:

1. Adam and Eve failed in the Garden of Eden (Gen. 2:16–17; 3:1–6).
2. Noah built the ark (Gen. 6:13–22).
3. Lot fled Sodom (Gen. 19:12–22).
4. Abraham was asked by God to sacrifice Issac (Gen. 22:1–14).
5. Moses failed as he struck the rock instead of commanding it at Meribah (Num. 20:6–13).
6. Samuel learned to listen to God and obey (1 Sam. 3:1–18).
7. David repented when challenged by Nathan (2 Sam. 12).
8. Solomon failed as he married foreign wives (1 Kings 11:1–13).
9. Levites failed to move the ark as God directed (1 Chron. 13: 9–11).

10. David gave personal assets for the building of a temple
    (1 Chron. 29:3, 5, 14).
11. Isaiah answered the call of God (Isa. 6:8).
12. Jonah failed when he refused to go to Nineveh (Jon. 1:1–3).
13. Daniel prayed and received an interpretation of the king's
    dream (Dan. 2:17–28).
14. Paul received a vision that he was to go to Macedonia (Acts
    16:9–10).
15. Philip followed the Holy Spirit's instructions and led an
    Ethiopian eunuch to the Lord (Acts 8:26–40).

Prayer Tests

If any of you lacks wisdom, he should ask God, who gives generously
to all without finding fault, and it will be given to him. But when he
asks, he must believe and not doubt, because he who doubts is like
a wave of the sea, blown and tossed by the wind.

James 1:5–6

Is any one of you sick? He should call the elders of the church to
pray over him and anoint him with oil in the name of the Lord. And
the prayer offered in faith will make the sick person well; the Lord
will raise him up. If he has sinned, he will be forgiven.

James 5:14–15

Ask and it will be given to you; seek and you will find; knock and
the door will be opened to you. For everyone who asks receives; he
who seeks finds; and to him who knocks, the door will be opened.
Which of you, if his son asks for bread, will give him a stone? Or
if he asks for a fish, will give him a snake? If you, then, though
you are evil, know how to give good gifts to your children, how
much more will your Father in heaven give good gifts to those
who ask him!

Matthew 7:7–11

In the hectic pace of ministry, vital communication with God via
prayer is often neglected. Prayer is one of the major character issues
that is constantly reemphasized by God. The prayer test may be stimu-
lated by pressing personal needs or ministry needs, but its essence is
more than the answer to those needs. It is a reminder that prayer is

a necessary leadership habit that enhances communication with God and secures vision for ministry.

Prayer tests refer to those instances when God reminds leaders that they must pray in order to have effective ministry. The ultimate goal of this test is to help the leader see prayer not as a burden but as a release, a privilege to be entered into joyfully.

Prayer tests usually involve a situation or need that is resolved or met through specific prayer. The prayer is answered in such a way that God's power and the authenticity of the leader's spiritual authority are clearly demonstrated.

Scriptural examples include:

1. God healed Abimelech's wife in answer to Abraham's prayer (Gen. 20:17–18).
2. Moses interceded for people of Israel (Exod. 32:11–14; Num. 14:13–23).
3. Hannah prayed for a son (1 Sam. 1:9–18).
4. Solomon asked for wisdom (1 Kings 3:5–14).
5. Elisha prayed for a dead boy (2 Kings 4:32–35).
6. Hezekiah prayed for help against the Assyrians (2 Kings 19:14–19).
7. Hezekiah prayed for the saving of his life (2 Kings 20:1–6).
8. Jehoshaphat prayed for the people of Israel in war (2 Chron. 20:12, 22).
9. Nehemiah prayed and received the favor of the king (Neh. 2:2–8).
10. Jonah prayed for God to save him when he was swallowed by a whale (Jon. 2:1–10).
11. Believers prayed in the upper room as they waited on the Holy Spirit (Acts 1–2).
12. Believers prayed in support of Peter and John (Acts 4:24–31).

Spiritual Power Tests

But I will harden Pharaoh's heart, and though I multiply my miraculous signs and wonders in Egypt, he will not listen to you.

Exodus 7:3–4

Men of Israel, listen to this: Jesus of Nazareth was a man accredited by God to you by miracles, wonders and signs, which God did among you through him, as you yourselves know.

Acts 2:22

So Paul and Barnabas spent considerable time there, speaking boldly for the Lord, who confirmed the message of his grace by enabling them to do miraculous signs and wonders.

Acts 14:3

Spiritual power tests are used by God to train a leader to appropriate God's power through faith. They usually involve the exercise or demonstration of the power of spiritual gifts where the leader uses a specific spiritual gift that clearly demonstrates the Holy Spirit's power. God's supernatural gifts are given so that leaders have the spiritual abilities necessary to lead.

Scriptural examples include:

1. Joseph interpreted dreams of Pharaoh but gave God all the credit (Genesis 41).
2. Moses confronted Pharaoh (Exodus 5–11).
3. Moses at Red Sea (Exod. 14:10–31).
4. Moses and the earthquake following Korah's rebellion (Num. 16:35).
5. The people of Israel crossed the Jordan River while the water stopped (Josh. 3:7–4:14).
6. The fall of Jericho (Joshua 6).
7. Samuel called down thunder and rain (1 Sam. 12:16–17).
8. Elijah and his encounter with the priests of Baal (1 Kings 18:17–40).
9. Elijah called for rain (1 Kings 18:41–46).
10. Elisha cured some deadly water (2 Kings 2:19–22).
11. Elisha healed Naaman (2 Kings 5:3–16).
12. Shadrach, Meshach, and Abednego in the furnace (Dan. 3:19–30).
13. Daniel in the lions' den (Dan. 6:10–28).
14. Philip in his ministry in Samaria (Acts 8:4–8).
15. Paul and Silas in a Philippian jail (Acts 16:25–34).

Spiritual Warfare Tests

For though we live in the world, we do not wage war as the world
does. The weapons we fight with are not the weapons of the world.
On the contrary, they have divine power to demolish strongholds. We
demolish arguments and every pretension that sets itself up against
the knowledge of God, and we take captive every thought to make
it obedient to Christ.

2 Corinthians 10:3–5

The seventy-two returned with joy and said, "Lord, even the de-
mons submit to us in your name." He replied, "I saw Satan fall like
lightning from heaven."

Luke 10:17–18

Spiritual warfare tests refer to those instances in ministry where the
leader discerns that ministry conflict is primarily supernatural in its
source and essence. He depends on God's power to solve the problem
in such a way that his leadership capacity, particularly his spiritual
authority, is demonstrated and expanded. This test occurs whether or
not a leader possesses the spiritual gift of discerning spirits. Those with
that gift will naturally see spiritual reality more quickly and recognize
spiritual warfare. All leaders, however, need the ability to discern spiritual reality in general and spiritual warfare in particular.

In some situations the leader may have to exercise or demonstrate
the power of God when there is confrontation between people representing God and people representing other supernatural forces.
The issue is power, and God's credibility is at stake. God vindicates
his credibility and the credibility of the leader as well in an unusual
demonstration of his power.

Scriptural examples include:

1. Elijah's confrontation with the prophets of Baal (1 Kings
   18:16–40).
2. Angels came to help Elisha and the army of Israel (2 Kings
   6:14–20).
3. Daniel waited upon God for the interpretation of a vision
   (Daniel 10).
4. Jesus was tempted in the wilderness (Matt. 4:1–11).
5. Paul was prevented from going to Thessalonica
   (1 Thess. 2:18).

Summary

Often when we are in the middle of a difficult trial in our life, it is hard to understand what we are going through and why. Sometimes we even lash out at God in anger for what we have to go through. However, at that point we might want to remember the story of Job. Notice what James said about Job: "As you know, we consider blessed those who have persevered. You have heard of Job's perseverance and have seen what the Lord finally brought about. The Lord is full of compassion and mercy" (James 5:11).

And yet this is the same Job we see contending with God about his situation. How is this an example of perseverance? First of all, Job recognized God was in the middle of the test. Second, he knew there was a reason for the test, but the explanations his friends were giving did not make sense. So he cried out to God for an opportunity to talk directly to God so he could understand God's purposes. Interestingly, when his request was granted, he was so overwhelmed by God's questions to him that he didn't say anything except to acknowledge the sovereignty of God in his life. We would do well to learn from Job and trust God in all circumstances.

There is no aspect of life where we can grow significantly without investing considerable effort, time, and difficult training. Students wish they didn't have to study and take tests, but that is part of the learning process. Athletes wish they didn't have to train and discipline themselves, but that is the only way they can excel. The same is true in our spiritual lives. If we learn our lessons well, even when we are facing difficult tests, we will significantly increase our personal happiness as well as our ministry effectiveness.

Questions for Reflection

1. As you have read through this chapter, what past experiences come to mind as significant tests (processes) that God was using to help you grow spiritually? How many of these did you recognize and acknowledge as tests (processes) that God was using to help shape your character?
2. Which growth processes (tests) identified in this chapter do you feel you have successfully completed?
3. Which growth processes (tests) identified in this chapter do you feel you have failed or have had a very difficult time learning?

7

THE COACHING
MODEL FOR CHRISTIAN
LEADERSHIP

- ■ LEADERSHIP CHARACTERISTICS OF
  EFFECTIVE COACHES
- ■ SUMMARY

We must rediscover our role as clergy, and it will probably be more
similar to the role of coach than that of chaplain or strong, authoritarian leader. As clergy, this means change. It means wrestling with
a new self-image of the pastoral role. It also means challenging our
congregations in their image of the pastoral role.[1]

Mike Regele

There are different categories of coaches. One extreme is the administrative coach, who makes sure that everything is in place so his
staff can coach the team. . . . Another type concentrates on a specific
aspect of the team and then surrounds himself with staff who coach
the other areas. . . . The coaches who have been the most successful
are usually the ones actively involved in the on-the-field, day-to-day
coaching. Players will sacrifice for a hands-on coach, because they
identify with him as an integral part of the team. A head coach who
sees his role only as motivating the team and organizing the staff

is at the mercy of other people. Having spent so many years as an assistant coach, I became more and more aware that someone had to be the source of game strategy and tactics.[2]

Bill Walsh

Despite the commonly held belief that every leader needs to be a good coach, leaders tend to exhibit this style least often.[3]

Daniel Goleman

Blaine had been an outstanding athlete at both high school and college levels. In fact, after he graduated from college he briefly considered a coaching career and even served as a volunteer assistant for one year while he finished a graduate degree. Upon graduating he went into a business career that was financially rewarding but personally unfulfilling. Finally he had a definite spiritual experience that he took to be a call of God on his life to enter ministry. The leaders in his church confirmed his calling, and he was asked to serve as an assistant pastor at his home church. However, his initial opportunities to minister proved as unfulfilling as had his secular job. It seemed as if there were constantly too many things to be done and too few people to do them.

Finally in desperation Blaine took a week off to reassess his goals and his careers. After a significant time of fasting and prayer, he was convinced he was to be in the ministry. So what was the problem? Blaine began to think back to his days as an athlete and coach and how excited he had been to participate and lead. Why wouldn't some of the same principles he saw work so successfully in coaching not work in the ministry? He began to view his role more as that of a coach than what he expected of himself as a pastor. Gradually the passion and excitement returned to his work. The more he read the Scriptures and meditated on their meaning, the more he could see many of the coaching principles at work in the leaders of the early church. Today he is often asked to speak to pastors about how he developed a "team" ministry and how he implemented his "coaching" approach to ministry.

As discussed in the previous chapter, the development of proper biblical character is foundational for Christian leadership. However, the focus cannot be solely on character development. The story of Moses gives us a good example of someone who demonstrated an extraordinary level of biblical character but struggled with many aspects of leadership behavior. In my personal experience as a consultant with churches, I have seen this pattern far too often. In order for the church to increase its health and effectiveness, it appears that many pastors and ministry leaders are going to have to learn some new leadership behaviors.

Probably no area of American life has attracted more attention than the athletic field. To be sure, much of what is heard, seen, and done has no redeeming value other than that of entertainment. But beneath the surface, particularly with successful teams, lie some very valuable principles that are transferable to any field, including ministry. Recently several famous coaches have written books aimed at corporate leaders, trying to demonstrate how the principles the coaches use for the playing field can apply to the operation of a business. Many of these principles of leadership are useful for pastors and ministry leaders today. And, not surprisingly, we find these same principles used by godly leaders throughout the Bible.

The coaching model seems to balance the need for strong, visionary leadership with significant team building. Coaches recognize that when the game starts, they will not be playing, only watching from the sidelines. Their job is to prepare the players so they will respond correctly regardless of the obstacles they may face.

The coaching model of leadership does not require a certain behavioral style. The key to remember here is that personality appears to be God-given, while leadership style is learned behavior. Regardless of personality style, all pastors can adopt a coaching style of leadership. Too many pastors falsely assume that the only kind of pastors who get things done are those with more directive or charismatic behaviors. The truth is that all behaviors have certain qualities that help us and certain qualities that hinder us as we learn to lead. Certainly a study of men and women leaders in the Scriptures does not give us a picture of God using only directive or charismatic behaviors.

You may remember from chapter 2 the DISC instrument published by Performax Systems International. They published another version of the same instrument that is titled "Biblical Personal Profiles." Below you will see a copy of the DISC chart we used in chapter 1 and some of the examples of Old and New Testament leaders that were identified with different personality styles. As you can see, God used all of the various personality styles in his selection of leaders.

Task Oriented Product Oriented Rational	C—Analyzer Moses Elijah David Luke	Controller—D Joshua Solomon Nehemiah Paul
People Oriented Process Oriented Emotional	Abraham Isaac Jacob John S—Supporter	Barnabas Peter Promoter—I
	Less Assertive/Verbal Tend to Respond	More Assertive/Verbal Tend to Initiate

We need to recognize that while the coaching model emphasizes certain common characteristics, there is also a lot of room for individuality. This allows leaders to be the people they were designed to be by God. Too many pastors and ministry leaders fail to take into account who they really are as they move into ministry. It only makes sense to take into account personal issues such as social and demographic background as well as talents and abilities when assuming a leadership position. Christian leaders should assume that God is the one who has been preparing them for leadership, and he has provided them with the background and tools necessary to lead. While they must continue to grow and develop additional skills, they should also try to understand who they are and how that fits into God's plan for leading others.

The coaching model of leadership touches on the deepest needs of an organization but at the same time sees the potential for the future. Coaches live in the tension between these two worlds. They must balance their time between meeting the needs of today and preparing for tomorrow. They recognize that for tomorrow to happen, they must initiate and lead today. If their leadership style is genuinely transformational, people will follow.

> The world of the 1990's and beyond will not belong to "managers" or those who can make the numbers dance. The world will belong to passionate, driven leaders—people who not only have enormous amounts of energy but who can energize those whom they lead.[4]
>
> Noel Tichy and Stratford Sherman

The drive to significance is a simple extension of the creative impulse of God that gave us being. . . . It is outwardly directed to the good to be done. We were built to count, as water is made to run downhill. We are placed in a specific context to count in ways no one else does. That is our destiny.[5]

Dallas Willard

Leadership Characteristics of Effective Coaches

If we believe that the coaching model has significant value for effective Christian leadership, then it makes sense to try and define what it is that effective coaches do. What characteristics separate successful coaches from those who are unsuccessful? What characteristics of effective coaches are transferable to other fields, particularly Christian ministry? Based on the empirical evidence I have gathered over thirty years of consulting, the following is a discussion of key distinctives of effective coaches that are consistent with foundational biblical principles.

Effective Coaches Initiate

A leader is, by definition, an innovator. He does things other people haven't done or don't do. He does things in advance of other people. He makes new things. He makes old things new. Having learned from the past, he lives in the present, with one eye on the future.[6]

Warren Bennis

This is leadership that transcends the mere management of what already exists, to create something fundamentally new. The field itself is new, a study not of heroes, but of the ways ordinary people can bring institutions through the convulsions of dramatic change.[7]

Noel Tichy

To lead is to go out ahead and show the way when the way may be unclear, difficult or dangerous.[8]

Robert K. Greenleaf

Leaders by definition are required to initiate, but coaches especially recognize their responsibility to start things, to step out in front. Good coaches are not afraid to put forth their ideas; they are willing to be proactive instead of reactive. The way they initiate may vary from one individual to another and from one situation to another, but the team expects them to be out in front, thinking ahead, and setting the pace.

Leaders simply must lead. That is the essence of leadership. They can't just follow along. They must step out in front. And if they do step out, and if people follow them, they can be considered leaders. "When the princes in Israel take the lead, when the people willingly offer themselves—praise the LORD!" (Judg. 5:2).

I love the following quote from Elmer Towns: "Many will follow a pastor with a vision not for rational reasons, but because the odds are against him and, in fact, appear insurmountable. The charismatic leader appeals to the deep feelings of the populace, and they hope he can somehow 'pull it off.'"[9]

The reasons proactive leadership seems to work so well in ministry settings are twofold:

- First, volunteers and lay leaders have little discretionary time on their hands. They appreciate a more proactive style that gives them some initial direction. They want to have input on major decisions, but they do not have the time to begin with blank sheets of paper when it comes to problem solving.
- Second, there is already too much managing and not enough leading. People prefer to be led by vision and direction rather than just policies and procedures. A more proactive leadership style implies leading, not just managing.

The Christian analogy most often used for the role of pastor or ministry leaders is that of shepherd. It is interesting that if we study the role of a shepherd as given in Scripture, we see him leading. Look at just a few Scriptures that describe Jesus' concept of leadership:

The man who enters by the gate is the shepherd of his sheep. The watchman opens the gate for him, and the sheep listen to his voice. He calls his own sheep by name and leads them out. When he has brought out all his own, he goes on ahead of them, and his sheep follow him because they know his voice. But they will never follow a stranger; in fact, they will run away from him because they do not recognize a stranger's voice.

John 10:2–5

They were on their way up to Jerusalem, with Jesus leading the way, and the disciples were astonished, while those who followed were afraid. Again he took the Twelve aside and told them what was going to happen to him.

Mark 10:32

Notice in the first passage, from the book of John, that Jesus identifies the true shepherd as one who "*leads them out*," and "*he goes ahead of them.*" The sheep follow not because they are coerced but because they know and trust the voice of the shepherd.

In the second passage, from the book of Mark, we see Jesus setting his face toward Jerusalem even though he knew he would be facing death there. Jesus led the way, and this astonished the disciples because they did not understand God's plan nor the courage of their leader, Jesus.

In the Old Testament Nehemiah demonstrated many of the attributes of a great leader, but he was particularly proactive. After hearing about the difficult conditions in Jerusalem, Nehemiah immediately began to fast and pray about the situation (Nehemiah 1). When he finally was able to present his case to the king (six months after he began praying), he had a carefully prepared plan (Neh. 2:7–8). After arriving in Jerusalem he personally surveyed the situation and came up with a more detailed plan of how he would accomplish his mission. From then until the walls of the city were rebuilt, we continually see Nehemiah stepping out in front to lead.

Unfortunately, one of the common misperceptions regarding leadership is that it implies autocratic, dictatorial, or abusive behavior. Nothing could be further from the truth. A range of behaviors falls under legitimate leadership, and some of these behaviors are more directive than others.

There is a danger that if leaders move too much toward directive behavior, they will become increasingly out of touch and abusive of those around them. We all have observed this type of leadership behavior, even in the church, and are dismayed by the fallout that occurs in these situations. Autocratic leadership behavior may work in the short-term or in emergency situations, but long-term autocratic leadership normally self-destructs.

True leadership, therefore, is not a mandate for autocratic leadership as some would say, but it clearly affirms the legitimate role of leaders to initiate. Joe Ellis distinguishes between authority and authoritarianism: "Authority and authoritarianism should not be confused. Authoritarianism says, 'This is right because I say so.' Authority says, 'I say this because it is right.' A good leader has authority on his side, but he is not an authoritarian."[10]

Effective Coaches Are Intentional

Effective coaches have a direction, a purpose, a reason for moving in a particular direction. They are not just going through the motions. They are seeking to accomplish specific objectives. The degree of clarity with which they see their destination may vary, but it is clear they are on a journey or a mission with specific outcomes in mind.

The church is no different. The apostle Paul is an example of someone who definitely was led by the Holy Spirit but was also intentional about his ministry. If you study Paul's missionary strategy in the book of Acts, you can see the depth of planning and organization that he used to accomplish his vision.

- **He had a definite plan of where he wanted to go and why.** He purposed to go to the areas where the gospel had not already been preached, and he organized his itinerary accordingly.
- **He never traveled alone.** Paul always took one or more individuals along with him (Barnabas and John Mark on his first journey; Silas, Timothy, and Luke on his second journey, etc.). His purpose was to mentor, disciple, and train others to fulfill the Great Commission, so that his work could be multiplied.
- **He had a definite strategy for taking cities.** Even though Paul had been commissioned as a messenger to the Gentiles, he went first to the local synagogues. While he did not shrink from testifying to the Jews assembled in those synagogues, his real target audience was the God-fearing Gentiles and proselytes who had attached themselves to the synagogue. He did this to maximize his effectiveness. He could have preached on any corner of town. But instead, he went where he knew he would find those who were most open and prepared to hear the gospel message. He also went where he knew he would be invited to speak. Usually within a short period of time Paul was forced out of these synagogues. He would then begin to meet with the new believers and their natural network of friends and relatives in one of their homes. These became the early churches.
- **He had a follow-up program.** Paul regularly sent his designated helpers to the churches to see how they were doing as well as to

encourage and exhort the believers in their faith. He also wrote letters to many of the churches, giving them instructions and answering their questions.

From the writings of Luke and Paul we see that while Paul was an intentional leader, he was flexible enough to change or adjust his plans when led by the Holy Spirit, delayed by Satan, or when ministering in different cultural contexts.

According to authors James Kouzes and Barry Posner, "We expect our leaders to have a sense of direction. . . . Leaders must know where they are going. They must have a destination in mind when asking us to join them on a journey into the unknown."[11]

This is the essence of good leadership. We must keep our eyes on our mission and vision but adjust our methods and strategies as necessary along the way. Paul's strategy and methodology clearly reflected the unique combination of his call, his training, and his context. The effectiveness of his efforts did not happen by accident.

Effective Coaches Develop, Transform, or Empower Others

A good leader can raise people to heights that they may have only imagined in daydreams and childhood aspirations.[12]

Alan Nelson and Stan Toler

No leader sets out to be a leader. People set out to live their lives expressing themselves fully. When that expression is of value, they become leaders. So the point is not to become a leader. The point is to become yourself, to use yourself completely—all your skills, your gifts and energies—in order to make your vision manifest. You must withhold nothing. You must, in sum, become the person you started out to be and to enjoy the process of becoming.[13]

Warren Bennis

One of the key motivations for getting into coaching is the opportunity to develop the potential in others. Coaches have a unique opportunity to accomplish personal objectives, but only if they get others to succeed. They cannot do it by themselves.

The same is true in ministry. The only way pastors and ministry leaders can genuinely accomplish their mission or vision is by and through others.

Leaders by definition have followers. They have people constantly around them who are as eager as the leader to accomplish the tasks at hand.

Empowerment, however, does not mean simply giving others power without direction. To do so would most likely mean failure for the team, since each person would only pursue his or her own personal goals, which might or might not be compatible with the others.

Great leaders realize that as they spend time strengthening others, the returns are multiplied many times over.

Jesus himself is the best example of an empowering leader. Obviously he could have spent his entire time of ministry just personally teaching and challenging the Jewish people. He didn't need to recruit and train disciples. And yet, that was the genius of his strategy. By spending time with the disciples, he empowered them to carry on his ministry after his death. While they would never have imagined what they would be doing, because of Jesus's ministry and leadership with them they were able to transform their world.

The apostle Paul is another outstanding example. Again, with his education and a personal visitation of the Lord, he certainly could have carried out his ministry by himself. But he realized that if he wanted to multiply his effectiveness, he needed to take the time to include others. He empowered those who traveled and ministered with him so that they were able to carry on his ministry even when he was in prison. Not only did the spread of the gospel message continue while Paul was in prison, it increased through the ministry of his disciples.

Everyone in a leadership role or position is required to lead. The real question is what type of leader he or she will be.

- A poor leader doesn't know the needs of his followers and therefore doesn't lead them anywhere.
- A good leader knows the needs of his followers and therefore leads them where they want to go.
- A great leader knows the needs of his followers that they don't even see yet and therefore leads them where they need to be.

Effective Coaches Believe in Excellence and Accountability

His master replied, "Well done, good and faithful servant! You have been faithful with a few things: I will put you in charge of many things. Come and share your master's happiness!"

Matthew 25:21

Success is a peace of mind which is the direct result of self-satisfaction in knowing that you did your best to become the best you are capable of becoming.[14]

John Wooden

Whether coaches like it or not, whether it is always fair or not, coaches are measured, graded, and evaluated regularly by the success or failure of their teams. The results of their coaching efforts are regularly measured and reported on a scoreboard or in the newspapers. While this criterion may not adequately represent all the things that a good coach is trying to do, wise coaches have their own evaluation techniques to measure the real success or failure of their efforts. Coaches develop specific plans and strategies to achieve what they have defined as success. These plans are flexible enough to be adjusted as necessary during the course of the game. However, it doesn't make any difference whether or not they want their performance to be measured, because when the game is played, the results are very public.

One of the problems in ministry is defining what we mean by "success." Every church ministry or program area needs to develop a clear picture of what part it plays in fulfilling the mission and vision of the church. In other words, it needs to define clearly what success is for its area of ministry. How will they know if they are fulfilling their part of the church's vision? It's amazing how few pastors and ministry leaders have any kind of definition of success and any way of keeping track of how they are doing.

Clearly defining what you are trying to accomplish as well as how you will measure progress ensures the necessary focus for effective ministry. Here's how:

- The leaders' energy and activity is on target and purposeful. They know exactly what they are trying to accomplish and why.
- The leaders know what effectiveness means. They have clearly defined and measurable criteria for success.
- All resources (time, people, and dollars) are used effectively and efficiently.
- Genuine accountability is possible through regular, systematic evaluation based on the success criteria.

The combination of all these factors means fruitfulness and effectiveness or, as we say in Christian circles, good stewardship.

But why must a pastor or church leader focus on effectiveness and accountability? The answer is found in the biblical principles related to stewardship.

- **Everything we have comes from God and belongs to him, not us.** As Christian leaders we have to decide if we really believe that everything we have belongs to God and has simply been entrusted to us for his purposes. This includes our talents, our abilities, our spiritual gifts, and even our ministry opportunities. If we believe our ministry is truly given to us as a trust, then we realize what an awesome responsibility it is to fulfill that assignment with excellence and passion.

- **We are held accountable to be good stewards (managers) of all that is entrusted to us and are expected to increase or bring a return on what we have been given.** As Jesus said in Luke 12:48, "From everyone who has been given much, much will be demanded; and from the one who has been entrusted with much, much more will be asked."

The Scriptures clearly teach that not only have we been entrusted with everything we have, we are expected to do something with what God has given us. In other words, God has given us our ministries with specific results in mind. While it is God who gives us all we need to fulfill our ministry assignments, we are expected to do our part. God wants us to learn to live disciplined and focused lives not only to take care of ourselves but to accomplish his purposes for our lives.

Striving for effective stewardship (or excellence) also implies two other key leadership behaviors:

- **Developing a reward system that is linked to clearly defined criteria for success.** It is important that the success criteria are jointly determined. I personally prefer to have those working on the team develop their criteria and then have the leader make sure that the criteria are consistent with the overall mission and vision as well as reasonable. Team members usually set the criteria too high for the first year and too low for longer-run objectives.

- **The leader takes the initiative to celebrate accomplishments along the way.** Many leaders forget this step because they are overly task focused. They are ready to get on to the next step, but most people need reinforcement in the form of recognition of achievement. This could mean recognizing individual achievement or team accomplishments, but it must be done well and also be genuine. Leaders are usually amazed at the impact these celebration events have on the morale of the team.

Effective pastors and ministry leaders not only know where they are going but are motivated to evaluate their progress. They hold themselves and others accountable to ensure they are moving in the intended direction. They see their leadership opportunities as something that has been entrusted to them, and they want to make sure they are successful in completing their assignment.

> Delegation without follow-through is abdication. You can never wash your hands of a task. Even after you delegate it, you are still responsible for its accomplishment, and monitoring the delegated task is the only practical way for you to ensure a result.
>
> Andrew Grove

In the example from the parable of the talents (Matt. 25:14–30; Luke 19:12–27), the manager commended the servants who took what they had been given and figured out ways to make it increase. He made an example of the one who simply held on to what he had been entrusted. The manager declared that what had been entrusted to this unworthy servant would be taken from him and given to the servant who would do something with it. This only makes sense because God is not going to waste his resources on us if he knows we will use them foolishly or, even worse, not use them at all.

The biggest difficulty in ministry is how to define success. It is easy to see the bottom line in business (How much money did we make?) or in coaching (Did we win the game?). But ministry doesn't lend itself to simple measurement. How, for example, do we measure our success in worship or prayer?

Most businesses today use more than "hard" measurements to determine their success (i.e., quantitative data). They also use "soft" measurements that are based on surveys and other forms of feedback (i.e., qualitative feedback). They attempt to find out what the customers feel and think of their products or business. We have the opportunity to do the same kind of data gathering in the church. While it is a bit uncomfortable at first, churches that have expanded their definition of measuring progress are finding it can be done.

Being genuinely accountable is a characteristic of all good Christian leaders. Even if others do not hold them accountable, they have high standards for themselves and are constantly evaluating how they are doing in fulfilling their God-given assignment.

Effective Coaches Are Good Communicators

It is not enough for leaders to have dreams of the future. They must be able to communicate these in ways that encourage us to sign on for the duration and to work hard toward the objective.[15]

James Kouzes and Barry Posner

I remember how scared I felt after sharing the vision. . . . I was overwhelmed with fear of failure. What if it doesn't happen? Is this vision really from God or is it just the wild dream of an idealistic twenty-six-year old? It was one thing to privately dream of what I expected God to do; it was another matter to publicly state that dream. In my mind, I had now passed the point of no return.[16]

Rick Warren

Paint a compelling picture of this vision in the minds and hearts of the people so as to catalyze them to work together to bring about God's plans for your ministry.[17]

Jim Dethmer

One characteristic of all good coaches is their ability to communicate effectively. Not all are born with this ability, but good coaches develop and sharpen their communication skills so they can share effectively with others. Again, they don't all do it the same way. There is plenty of room for individuality in the communication process. But good coaches start out with the assumption that in order to operate successfully in a team environment, you had better learn to communicate both individually and corporately.

Having passion about what you are sharing provides a great start for effective communication. Making sure that you communicate through your natural behavioral style is another. However, empirical research in the field of communications has revealed that the number one criterion for effective communication is credibility.[18] Leaders who rate highly on the dimensions of trustworthiness, expertise, and dynamism are considered to be more credible sources of information.

This is one area where Christian leaders should have a significant advantage. And yet, because of the public failures of several Christian leaders in the area of personal or moral integrity, many Christian leaders find themselves fighting an uphill battle for credibility.

Not surprisingly, successful ministry is based on credibility. That is why it is so hard when a church suffers moral failure within the leadership team. Trust disappears quickly and is very difficult to reestablish. Once a person feels betrayed by a leader, it takes a long time to win back that trust and confidence.

Pastors and ministry leaders realize that they must learn to communicate effectively on a number of levels, just like coaches. They must be good in one-on-one communication, small-group or team communication, and often in public settings with a large crowd. Successful pastors and ministry leaders learn early on that to communicate effectively, you must learn to use illustrations, be able to tell stories, and have a sense of humor. These are skills that can be learned, but they don't just happen automatically.

Effective Coaches Provide Visionary Leadership

It is clear that the majority of us can agree on what we want from our leaders. We want them to be credible, and we want them to have a sense of direction. If someone is to lead us, that person must be able to stand before us and confidently express an attractive image of the future, and we must be able to believe that he or she has the ability to take us there.[19]

James Kouzes and Barry Posner

We need people who influence their peers and who cannot be detoured from their convictions by peers who do not have the courage to have any convictions.[20]

Joe Paterno

Effective coaches must have a clear picture of where they are trying to take the team and then model what they believe. Having vision is having a compelling picture of a preferred future. All good coaches have vision. This vision is a concise and clear picture that is based on key assumptions and values formed in the heart of the leader.

The most common biblical reference used to support the need for vision is the King James Version of Proverbs 29:18: "Where there is no vision, the people perish." However, the NIV has a slightly different interpretation, "Where there is no revelation, the people cast off restraint." This reminds us of the biblical analogy of Christians as sheep and the church as a flock. Flocks of sheep need shepherds to guide, protect, and give them direction. Without shepherds, the sheep will become *unrestrained*, either running off and getting hurt or turning on one another and fighting. What a sad but accurate picture of a church that lacks the necessary leadership and vision. Where there is no direction, no dream, nothing beyond self-preservation and maintaining the status quo to guide us, we run off and get hurt or turn on one another.

> The mission has to be clear and simple. It has to be bigger than any one person's capacity. It has to lift up people's vision. It has to be something that makes each person feel that he or she can make a difference—that each one can say, I have not lived in vain.[21]
>
> Peter Drucker

Discovering God's vision for our future is not a fad. It is not something brand-new, neither is it something that is going to pass away.

> "For I know the plans I have for you," says the LORD. "They are plans for good and not for disaster, to give you a future and a hope."
>
> Jeremiah 29:11

Many have wondered why it is so important to capture a specific vision for the church or for a ministry. Perhaps the simplest answer is that if we don't have a picture of where we are going we will likely end up somewhere else. If a farmer wants to plow a straight furrow, he cannot look at the ground immediately in front of him; he needs to focus farther on, on some point at the end of the field or on the horizon. That point provides direction and guidance and keeps him going in a straight line, rather than wandering all over.

Businesses have discovered that it's not enough merely to have a great product or even a great location. The number of new businesses that fail each year is a testimony to the difficulty of surviving in a very competitive marketplace. And the opposite is also true. Many of the truly great companies in the United States today were started by men and women who overcame unbelievably difficult circumstances and yet not only survived but also thrived in the same market setting. Those who have researched these successes and failures point to the essential role that vision or lack of vision played in the outcomes of these companies.

In the athletic arena we see the same thing. The differences in athletic ability between professional teams are truly minimal. And yet we see certain teams that continue to dominate, while others continue to fail. Studies have shown that it is not the team that always spends the most amount of money or even has the most talented athletes that stays at the top. Instead, books written by coaches and players alike point to the intangibles and in particular the vision of the coach or organization that made the difference.

> If you stacked these teams up against one of the perennial contenders, the talent gap might not be as great as you'd expect. It's the philosophy gap that separates them. The losers lack something vital: a sense of purpose.[22]
>
> Bill Parcells

In my own empirical research on church health and effectiveness, I have found no factor more important than what could be termed vision. And yet we see very little written about this concept in contemporary Christian books. We see little, if anything, taught about it in our seminaries and Bible colleges. And in fact, if a pastor wants to learn about vision, he will have to turn primarily to books from the business and athletic fields. It reminds me of Luke 16:8: "For the people of this world are more shrewd in dealing with their own kind than are the people of the light."

Vision is the first and most essential tool for leaders to have. Without a vision leaders would have nowhere to go, nowhere to point to, and nowhere to lead.

> After the completion of Disney World, someone remarked, "Isn't it too bad that Walt Disney didn't live to see this!" Mike Vance, creative director of Disney Studios replied, "He did see it—that's why it's here."[23]
>
> From *Ministry Advantage*

> Far better to dare mighty things, to win glorious triumphs, even though checkered by failure, than to take rank with those poor spirits

who neither enjoy much nor suffer much, because they live in the gray twilight that knows not victory, nor defeat.[24]

Theodore Roosevelt

Effective Coaches Motivate with Passion

Every man is enthusiastic at times. One man has enthusiasm for 30 minutes, another for 30 days, but it is the man who has it for 30 years who makes a success of his life.[25]

Walter Cottingham

In short, few start-ups—inside the corporation or out—succeed without passion. (Many passionate entrepreneurs fail. But that's not the point. Almost none succeed without passion.) The odds are stacked so high against the entrepreneur that only irrational commitment—i.e., passion, emotion—stands even a chance of carrying the day.[26]

Tom Peters

One of the biggest differences between coaches and other types of leaders is their passion for what they do. Coaches are excited about what they do and are not afraid to show it. In fact, they couldn't coach without it. True, they demonstrate it in different ways. Some are much more vocal and demonstrative, but all would agree that emotion and passion are an essential part of their coaching strategy.

Enthusiasm can be contagious. People are looking for leaders who are passionate about their work. They are looking for leaders who really care about what they are doing. To be effective, passion must be genuine and used in a positive manner. Passionate leaders help focus team members on the right targets and get them moving in a positive direction. There are a lot of internal and external motivating factors, but passion seems to be one that universally motivates individuals as well as groups of people.

Leaders naturally gravitate toward opportunities where there is a certain level of risk. The risk is part of what motivates them. They are not afraid of failing but see temporary setbacks as a natural part of the learning curve.

You cannot help but get excited when you read what the apostle Paul said about his mission. The passion he expressed was certainly a response to what God had done for him but also to the opportunities

God had placed before him. There were times when he was definitely down and discouraged, but those were far outnumbered by the times when he was "driven" to accomplish the purposes for which God called him. The heavenly boldness that was part of Paul's leadership style was a key part in making him the great leader that he was. Listen to his passion in this quote from 1 Corinthians: "Do you not know that in a race all the runners run, but only one gets the prize? Run in such a way as to get the prize. Everyone who competes in the games goes into strict training. They do it to get a crown that will not last; but we do it to get a crown that will last forever. Therefore I do not run like a man running aimlessly; I do not fight like a man beating the air. No, I beat my body and make it my slave so that after I have preached to others, I myself will not be disqualified for the prize" (1 Cor. 9:24–27).

Effective Coaches Develop Teams

It's amazing how much can be accomplished if no one cares who gets the credit.[27]

Blanton Collier

Leadership in these churches is team leadership and most pastors are unskilled in this approach and yet it is much more fun. . . . The church is much less likely to crater if the pastor leaves because the pastor is one member of a team.[28]

George Hunter

Few coaches are player coaches. Most spend their time coaching others and allowing players to play. The primary role of the coach is to ensure the overall development of the team.

In trying to assess the popularity of sports in America, particularly among young people, one of the factors often overlooked is the relationships developed in a team environment. Training together, working together on common goals, succeeding and failing together are factors that create a genuine team environment.

Team chemistry is often overlooked in sports but is usually one of the first things mentioned by athletes who participate on winning teams. Also cited is the leadership role of the coach or coaches.

Great leaders recognize that they must enlist others and get them to work together. Both functions take a lot of time. Recruiting the right people is a big part of leadership responsibility. To be an excellent recruiter, you must be able to see what the person will be like in the future, not what they are now.

Once you have recruited the right people, they have to learn to work together. Too many leaders assume this happens automatically. It doesn't, particularly in our culture. While we like to use terms like "collaboration," "networking," and "sharing," these terms become illusive when faced with the reality of ministry.

In the last fifteen years we have seen a phenomenal increase in the number of small groups or cell groups in churches across America. The popularity of this format appears to be driven by a desire for intimacy and personal bonding that people cannot get in church services. They want to have a supportive environment in which they can grow, share, and learn. Interestingly, there is a growing amount of evidence that many people who joined small groups are now dropping out. The number one reason people are dropping out of small groups is the lack of necessary leadership in the group. So, while the size of the group has some natural advantages for relationships, there is still a real need for quality leadership, even at this level.

Teams are not only valuable for relationships but also for task accomplishment. Research attests to the value of teams for achieving results. While not true in every single case, the general rule is that teams perform far better than the individuals could do by themselves. Thus the development of teams is a highly effective strategy for accomplishing significant results. The reason for the success appears to be the interaction of the group members. Having people with different personalities and different perspectives adds value for all involved.

How should we define what we mean by a team? Perhaps the best definition I have seen is one put forth by Don Simmons: "It's an enthusiastic group of people with complementary skills and gifts who work together toward common purposes and have a high level of trust and accountability."[29]

As we look at the success of the early church in the book of Acts, it is obvious that it was not just the work of a few extraordinary individuals. In fact, from the very beginning we see that many were very ordinary people, as mentioned in 4:13: "When they saw the courage of Peter and John and realized that they were unschooled, ordinary men, they were astonished and they took note that these men had been with Jesus."

What was the key to their power besides the obvious spiritual power operating through them? They had been part of an incredible team trained by Jesus himself. We often fail to appreciate how unusual Jesus's strategy was to touch the world with the gospel message. If we knew we had to reach the entire world and our ministry would only last approximately three years, what would be our strategy? We would probably try to gather the largest groups possible and try to touch the most people in the shortest period of time. The strategy of Jesus was entirely different. He chose to spend an inordinate amount of time with twelve disciples whom he recruited, trained and equipped, deployed, and monitored. While initially they were very common men, by the time they had spent three years with Jesus, they were changed men in more ways than one.

Today there is a strong move in business circles toward team development. While it may be one of the business fads that come and go, there certainly is enough research to support the high value of teams even in a business venue. Much of the creativity that we see, particularly in the high-tech field, is the result of team development. While there are still "superstars" in business like there are in any field, even most of those men and women have discovered the benefits of surrounding themselves with teams of people who can help execute the business plan.

While small groups have become common in churches, the same cannot be said in regard to ministry leadership. Whether you are talking about pastoral leadership, lay leadership, or ministry leadership, most of what takes place is individual ministry rather than team ministry. The odd thing is that most ministry leaders complain about how tired they are and how frustrated they are at the amount of work that they have to do personally. The answer would seem to be to reestablish genuine team ministry. And the essential key in developing these teams is developing better leaders.

For whatever reason, most pastors have a lone-ranger approach to ministry. They feel a need to do everything themselves. And this model is passed down to other pastors and ministry leaders. While on paper there may be teams at the ministry level, members of these teams will generally tell you there is little genuine team ministry. This is another reason why the church is seeing a decline in volunteers. People want to do ministry and use their spiritual gifts, but they want to do it along with others. They want to be part of a team. When they move into ministry, many are disappointed to find little support or team camaraderie. It's unfortunate because, as Ecclesiastes 4:9–12 says, "Two are better than one, because they have a good return for their work: If one falls down, his friend can help him up. But pity the man who falls and has no one to help him up! Also, if two lie down together, they will keep warm. But how can one keep warm alone?

Though one may be overpowered, two can defend themselves. A cord of three strands is not quickly broken."

Effective Coaches Mentor, Train, and Equip

Coaches understand the necessity of having a process in place to improve the skills of both staff and players. Most of the training takes place in on-the-job training rather than in classroom settings. There is a strong commitment to go-and-grow versus sit-and-soak.

A major part of this commitment to training and equipping is the concept of multiplication. Just as most coaches see a significant turnover of athletes each year, most churches also experience a great deal of change. Only those ministry leaders committed to multiplying and reproducing other leaders are going to be able to keep pace and have the necessary numbers of leaders in place.

Coaches know that unless they develop and properly use the athletes on their team, they have little opportunity for success. As a result, they intentionally plan how they can best develop these athletes. We have several examples in Scripture of how leaders developed people around them, including Paul, Nehemiah, and Jesus.

THE APOSTLE PAUL

If you study the ministry of Paul, it is obvious that he valued the development of a team ministry. He never traveled alone and always took people along with him (Barnabas and Mark on his first missionary journey; Silas, Timothy, and Luke on his second; and Titus on his third). In some cases they just watched him minister. But in other situations we see them beginning to minister based on the training they received. Whenever Paul ministered for any length of time in a city, he usually developed a team around him. Priscilla and Aquila in Corinth are but one example. Many of these who traveled with Paul or ministered under his tutelage later became significant leaders in the early church. Even though Paul spent considerable time in prison for his faith, his fellow workers were able to carry on the important work of expanding the church and providing the necessary leadership and exhortation to the emerging churches.

NEHEMIAH

The book of Nehemiah is another outstanding example of the development of people around a good leader. Nehemiah not only grieved

THE COACHING MODEL FOR CHRISTIAN LEADERSHIP

over the reports he had received about conditions in Jerusalem, he not only prayed, he also planned. And he continued to demonstrate this planning ability as well as his leadership skills when he arrived in Jerusalem to lead in the rebuilding of the walls.

From the third chapter of Nehemiah we can see the division of labor Nehemiah used to rebuild the walls of Jerusalem. He was able to visualize how a massive project could be subdivided into smaller segments. The result was that through the efforts of these smaller units, each doing their task, the wall was completed in just fifty-two days. Good leaders are able to see the big picture but also how to break it down into bite-sized pieces so the work does not become overwhelming for those involved.

JESUS

The model of Jesus's own ministry is probably the best example of team ministry. Robert Coleman described Jesus's plan in his book *The Master Plan of Evangelism*: "There was nothing haphazard about His life—no wasted energy, not an idle word. He was on business for God (Luke 2:49). He lived, He died, and He rose again according to schedule. Like a general plotting His course of battle, the Son of God calculated to win. He could not afford to take a chance. Weighing every alternative and variable factor in human experience, He conceived a plan that would not fail."[30]

Pastor Gene Getz did an interesting study of the Scriptures, trying to determine how Jesus spent his time.[31] His conclusions are extremely interesting. Notice two incredible facts:

- Jesus spent an inordinate amount of time among people who would be considered either neutral or negative to his message (approximately 46 percent).
- Jesus spent an incredible amount of time with his disciples, either personally or as a group (approximately 39 percent).

Notice also Jesus's strategy in training and equipping his disciples.

- **He chose to focus and concentrate his ministry on a few.**
  Although Jesus had a large public teaching ministry, a significant portion of his time was spent training and equipping only a few men, his twelve disciples. While the demands on his time were

incredible, he made sure he spent the necessary time with those who would carry on his ministry after his ascension.

- **He had a specific training plan.** Jesus followed a very careful training format of: (1) Teaching the disciples the basic principles of ministry through parables, illustrations, and focused teaching; (2) Doing the ministry himself with the disciples watching; (3) Having the disciples do ministry with him coaching them; (4) Releasing the disciples to do ministry on their own. Interestingly, most of the training was on-the-job, not sit-and-soak.

- **He taught the disciples how to reproduce themselves.** He showed the disciples that what he was teaching and training them was not for them alone. he expected them to fulfill the Great Commission by training and equipping others. While the concept was difficult for many to grasp, we do see the early church spreading the gospel into the entire world.

It would certainly appear that Jesus did not expect perfection from his team. He had to demonstrate a great deal of tolerance. And we also see from the example of Judas that while we can work with people all we want, if their hearts are not willing to follow and learn, they won't, regardless of the leader.

When we think about it, Jesus's strategy was risky. Leaving the church in the hands of twelve ordinary men could have meant disaster. But it was exactly what Jesus had planned. And with the teaching and training he gave them, these disciples proved faithful in advancing the kingdom.

We would do well to learn from Paul, Nehemiah, and Jesus the importance of coaching others and developing teams.

Churches cannot wait for outside agencies (e.g., Bible colleges, seminaries, and parachurch ministries) to train their leaders for them. They must aggressively begin to fulfill the assignment of Ephesians 4:11–13. The following are some principles that will help in designing the training process for new leaders.

- Training must emphasize the practical aspects of personal and church ministry—training needs to be based on the skill sets and character qualities that are determined to be necessary to function successfully.

- Part of any training must be an understanding of how God trains and equips leaders, how God processes those who desire to become leaders.
- The focus of the training must be on go-and-grow, not sit-and-soak.
- Training must reflect and support the unique values and vision of the local church. Thus, any training that includes materials from other churches or parachurch ministries needs to be rewritten or adapted to the unique culture of the local church.
- Before any training begins instructors must be able to identify for each lesson what they want participants to know, what they want them to feel, and what they want them to do.
- Training must include the best uses of technology.
- Training must give participants the biblical foundation that supports the training.
- Training must be interactive. Sufficient time needs to be programmed into the training for questions and answers.
- Training must provide time and opportunity for practical application and practice. This could take many forms including role play, practical assignments to be completed between or after sessions, homework assignments, and so on, but must be included as a part of every lesson.
- Training must provide a mentoring process whereby participants can have someone they can go to with ongoing questions and problems. The mentor would oversee the implementation phase where the participants take what they have learned and apply it in a personal or ministry setting.
- Participants need to have multiple options for taking the training (e.g., intensive sessions, once-a-week sessions, and Internet-based training).
- There must be accountability for both participants and instructors. Evaluation of the results of the training as well as the participants' response to the training must be carefully assessed.
- Leaders need to continue reproducing themselves in the lives of others. It is assumed that anyone who is trained to lead will train and equip others.
- Leaders work in teams. It is assumed that anyone who is trained will develop a team around him or her to do the work of ministry.

Think of the situation in the early church. The book of Acts tells us that on the day of Pentecost, over three thousand new believers were added to the kingdom. This was a serious problem if you think of it in terms of how they were going to provide the necessary teaching, training, and equipping for all these new believers. And yet we see that not only were they able to do it, those who were trained and equipped were able to go out and spread the gospel significantly.

How did the early church train and equip leaders? It wasn't primarily by classes; it was primarily by mentoring or on-the-job training. The assumption was that leaders were to reproduce leaders who in turn would reproduce other leaders.

When we look at the ministry of Paul, Nehemiah, Jesus, and others, it's clear what the training and equipping process was.

- These leaders personally recruited potential leaders.
- They spent quality time together developing significant relationships.
- They taught the basic principles of ministry through parables, illustrations, and focused teaching.
- They did the ministry themselves with the trainees watching.
- They allowed the trainees to do the ministry while they coached them.
- They released the trainees to do ministry on their own.

Coaches spend countless hours planning how best to develop the athletes on their teams. They analyze the strengths and weaknesses of each member of the team and then develop specific plans for individual training as well as team drills and practice. They spend additional time supervising individual and team development. All of this takes place before any competition begins. The time of preparation far exceeds the actual time of playing the game. Pastors and ministry leaders could learn a great deal from the training and equipping practices of the best coaches.

Effective Coaches Have a Positive Expectation for the Future

A pessimist is one who makes difficulties of his opportunities; an optimist is one who makes opportunities out of his difficulties.[32]

Harry Truman

Coaches are eternal optimists. They always think there is a way to win. They spend countless hours planning and strategizing in order to have the best chance to succeed. They see defeat as a temporary setback and look forward to the opportunity to compete again when they can experience success.

One of the key differences between effective leaders and leaders that fail is how they view the world around them.

Martin Seligman wrote a significant book a few years ago titled *Learned Optimism*. The author summed up his research and observations as follows: "The defining characteristic of pessimists is that they tend to believe bad events will last a long time, will undermine everything they do, and are their own fault. The optimists, who are confronted with the same hard knocks of this world, think about misfortune in the opposite way. They tend to believe defeat is just a temporary setback, that its causes are confined to this one case. The optimists believe defeat is not their fault: Circumstances, bad luck, or other people brought it about. Such people are unfazed by defeat. Confronted by a bad situation, they perceive it as a challenge and try harder."[33]

Seligman found three areas where the difference between pessimists and optimists was most apparent: permanence, pervasiveness, and personalization. The differences were clearly demonstrated in two kinds of situations, times of failure and in times of success.[34]

REACTIONS TO FAILURE

Permanence: Pessimistic people believe that bad events are permanent and will persist. Optimistic people believe that bad events are temporary.

Pervasiveness: Pessimistic people believe that bad events are pervasive, that bad things are going to happen in every area of their life. Optimistic people believe that bad events are specific and don't mean anything beyond the actual event itself.

Personalization: Pessimistic people believe that bad events are their fault. Optimistic people can often see that bad events are not their fault but the fault of others.

The first important step in weathering failure is learning not to personalize it—making sure you know that your failure does not make you a failure.[35]

John Maxwell

Tell yourself, I'm not a failure. I failed at doing something. There's a big difference.[36]

Erma Bombeck

REACTIONS TO SUCCESS

Permanence: Optimistic people believe that success is very likely to persist. Pessimistic people believe that success is only temporary and disaster is around the corner.

Pervasiveness: Optimistic people believe that success is pervasive and that good things are going to happen in every area of their life. Pessimistic people believe that good events are specific and don't mean anything beyond the actual event itself.

Personalization: Optimistic people believe that success is the result of their effort. Pessimistic people feel that success has nothing to do with their own efforts but is mostly dependent on what others do.

Seligman's research showed that optimists were usually much more successful in whatever they were doing compared to the pessimists.

Those in the church should have more reason for being optimistic than those in the world. We have been given the gift of eternal life. We have been indwelt by the Holy Spirit. We have been given spiritual gifts with which to minister. And we have God continually working in our lives to produce the natural fruit that should come as a result of our relationship with him. With all these advantages, we should be eternal optimists. Perhaps a more scriptural term for what we should be is "overcomers": "For everyone born of God overcomes the world. This is the victory that has overcome the world, even our faith. Who is it that overcomes the world? Only he who believes that Jesus is the Son of God" (1 John 5:4–5).

Effective Coaches Understand the Roles of Team Chemistry and Momentum

Coaches understand that in order for teams to be successful and remain successful, two vital elements must normally be in place—positive team chemistry and positive momentum.

TEAM CHEMISTRY

Anyone who has coached a team can testify that how players interact with one another definitely affects how the team performs. While there are exceptions, generally speaking the more harmonious the players are with one another and the more positively they feel about one another, the better they perform. Dissension and divisiveness among players is usually both a sign of problems as well as an indicator of future problems. Some coaches inherit a group of athletes that have a better initial chemistry than others. But the best coaches are able to improve and maintain positive team chemistry. They see this as one of their main functions. In order to do this they must stay close to their players and understand what motivates them and how they are doing personally. Good coaches spot potential problems before they spread and address them as quickly as possible. They realize that the emotional well-being of their team members is a critical part of their coaching responsibility. Coaches even plan activities to help improve team chemistry and morale.

It reminds us very much of the role of the shepherd and his flock of sheep. The good shepherd is continually evaluating the condition of his flock and making sure that all of the sheep are healthy and as content as possible: "Be sure you know the condition of your flocks, give careful attention to your herds; for riches do not endure forever, and a crown is not secure for all generations" (Prov. 27:23–24).

The analogy of a flock is often used with a church, and pastors and ministry leaders are analogous to shepherds. That is why effective Christian leaders realize that they must understand the condition of those entrusted to them. Much of the church conflict we see today is the result of poor leadership or at least leadership that did not respond at the appropriate time or in the appropriate way. By constantly monitoring the "chemistry" and "morale" of their flock, they can adjust their leadership as necessary to increase effectiveness for themselves and those they lead.

MOMENTUM

Coaches understand that in every game there is an ebb and flow of emotion and energy that is constantly moving in one direction or another. The most successful coaches learn appropriate strategies to address negative momentum (thereby limiting its impact) and take advantage of positive momentum (thereby getting the maximum benefit possible). When momentum is positive, coaches find they can accomplish significantly more with less energy. They know that if they use these opportunities properly, they can significantly increase their effectiveness.

Christian leaders face the same issues. There is a constant ebb and flow in ministry. Christian leaders who learn to recognize these swings of momentum and take them into consideration in their leadership efforts are rewarded with increased success. Devising basic strategies for ministry is one part of the equation, but adjusting those strategies based on the degree of momentum in the ministry is equally important.

Effective Coaches Are Excellent Problem Solvers

Effective coaches are well known for their ability to solve problems and deal with adverse circumstances. They don't wait until problems come before planning alternative strategies. They anticipate problems and prepare themselves to deal with these problems. This is one characteristic that not only separates effective coaches from ineffective coaches but also separates effective and ineffective leaders in any field.

Almost anyone can succeed in favorable circumstances, when everything is going well. But what do you do when things don't go as planned or when you encounter major obstacles? Effective coaches think about and plan for these circumstances. For example, effective coaches have plans prepared ahead of time for what they will do if any of their key players gets hurt and cannot play. They have a backup person already trained and equipped to step in and take over. While they would prefer to have their number one person on the playing field, they are prepared if they have to go to number two.

Ministry can be somewhat deceptive when it comes to problems. Some think there should not be any problems because it is God's responsibility to take care of all the problems that his people have. That is the ultimate example of sticking your head in the sand, and example after example in the Scriptures disproves this view. Others recognize that problems will occur but fail to prepare for them because they see preparation as unspiritual or as beginning a self-fulfilling prophecy. The problem is that when the troubles come, these leaders are unprepared and usually are sidetracked as they attempt to deal with the problem in a reactive instead of a proactive manner.

Conflict and problems are a genuine part of ministry. It is how we deal with them that is spiritual or unspiritual, redemptive or destructive. Effective leaders are not overwhelmed by negative circumstances. In fact, effective leaders demonstrate their leadership skills best in these circumstances.

One of the things I have seen over and over in ministry is that God gives his leaders advance warning regarding problems that are ahead. It may be part of the spiritual gift mix of leaders, or it may simply be

God's intervention to help the leaders carry out their responsibilities. Unfortunately, many of God's leaders choose to ignore these warnings or to wait too long before they begin responding. By the time they do act, it is too late and the problems have become destructive. When leaders get these types of warnings, they should immediately begin praying regarding the issues and then watch to see God's confirmation of what is really going on. They should begin to ask for God's wisdom in how to deal with the situation and begin making plans accordingly.

Summary

By observing and modeling the behavior of successful coaches, we can learn a great deal about effective leadership behavior. The coaching characteristics discussed in this chapter are based on common leadership patterns of successful coaches. Obviously every successful coach does not exhibit all of these characteristics, nor do successful coaches demonstrate each characteristic exactly the same way. But effective coaches do demonstrate considerable strength in relation to many of these characteristics. Therefore, as you review these characteristics and compare them to your own leadership behavior, do not become discouraged. They simply represent a good checklist of effective leadership behaviors. You may find some that you are presently using, and if so, you can be encouraged to continue these behaviors. You will find others that you are not currently using but are intriguing for future development. These can become a conscious focus as you work on further developing your leadership skills.

Questions for Reflection

1. On the left side of a piece of paper, list the qualities identified in this chapter as leadership characteristics of effective coaches. On the right side, rate yourself on each characteristic using the following scale.

   - **Significantly Above Average**—You are presently exercising these qualities with ease and regularity.
   - **Above Average**—You exercise these qualities sometimes but feel there is a lot of room for growth and improvement.

- **Average**—Sometimes you exercise these qualities; sometimes you don't.
- **Below Average**—You occasionally exercise these qualities, but they are not normally exhibited.
- **Significantly Below Average**—You seldom or never exercise these qualities.

2. Which if any of the leadership characteristics of effective coaches listed in this chapter would you like to develop as part of your own leadership practices? How will you accomplish this?
3. Using the scale developed by Gene Getz, how do you use your time compared to how Jesus used his time? What are the implications?
4. Which of the training principles identified in this chapter are currently a part of the training process for leaders in your church?
5. Which of the training principles identified in this chapter are not currently a part of the training process for leaders in your church but need to be? How will you implement the changes?

8

DESIGNING
A PERSONAL
DEVELOPMENT PLAN

- ■ RECOGNIZING THE NEED FOR CHANGE
- ■ CELEBRATE THE PAST
- ■ CREATING A NEW FUTURE
- ■ MAKING CHANGE A REALITY
- ■ SUMMARY

A study conducted at the Weatherhead School of Management of Case Western Reserve University by Professor Jane Wheeler found that people who had developed learning agendas, those who tried out their new skills with many different people and spheres of their lives—not just at work, but also with family, church, and community groups, and so on—improved the most. And those improvements were still apparent up to two or more years later.[1]

Daniel Goleman

Old leaders can learn new tricks. Leaders can and do make significant, in some cases life-altering, changes in their styles that ripple into their teams and trigger important changes throughout the entire organization. . . . Although people may differ in the initial level of their natural abilities, everyone can learn to improve, no matter where he or she starts out. . . . Great leaders . . . are made as they gradually acquire, in the course of their lives and careers, the competencies that make them so effective. The competencies can be learned by any leader, at any point.[2]

Daniel Goleman

A personal plan for leadership development is important because, as we said earlier, effective leaders must be focused, intentional, and proactive. We have a critical role to play in our own development process. We must be active participants. This speeds up the process and brings significantly better results. While this is not just a onetime event, the principles that govern the development cycle are the same. Designing a personal development plan is similar to the strategic planning efforts done by churches and businesses but with a personal emphasis or focus.[3]

Change is difficult for most of us. And yet the reality is that to significantly increase our effectiveness and fruitfulness as Christian leaders, all of us will need to make some significant changes. There appears to be three major phases that every individual needs to go through in the process of personal change.

Recognizing the Need for Change

Everyone is influenced by his or her past. But as Christians, none of us has to be controlled by it.[4]

John Trent

Consider it pure joy, my brothers, whenever you face trials of many kinds, because you know that the testing of your faith develops perseverance. Perseverance must finish its work so that you may be mature and complete, not lacking anything.

James 1:2–4

Change requires motivation and that motivation normally comes from an internal sense of dissatisfaction with the way things are. When we are satisfied, there is no impetus for change, but when we are dissatisfied, we are much more open to change. Sometimes we become dissatisfied simply by our circumstances, by ministry failure, or by ministry conflict. But it doesn't make sense that we should have to wait for these types of negative events before we get the necessary motivation for change. So how can we create that sense of personal dissonance that will motivate us toward change?

Self-Assessment

What I lack is to clear in my mind what I am to do, not what I am to know. . . . The thing is to understand myself, to see what God really wished me to do . . . to find the idea for which I can live and die.[5]

Søren Kierkegaard

The first step is to take the time to do a serious self-evaluation. This is somewhat like a doctor's checkup. While we usually put it off because we are afraid of the results, eventually we realize the need to find out how we are really doing. While doing a serious self-assessment can be intimidating, it is an absolute necessity. Otherwise we may start in the wrong place or begin working on the wrong things. Defining current reality is the critical first step. Having accurate and reasonably objective information about our current situation provides the best baseline for change and growth.

There are at least three areas of personal assessment that are beneficial for Christian leaders. Each of these can be done by yourself or with the help of others around you. A combination of both is ideal. If you choose to include others in your self-evaluation, you need to select carefully. They must be people whom you trust, people with whom you already have a significant relationship, and people that have seen you operate in a leadership setting on multiple occasions.

Having people from different perspectives assist you in your self-evaluation process provides increased objectivity. However, you should be warned that it is not unusual to get some conflicting information when you ask for others' observations. Remember that any given person only sees a certain part of your leadership behavior, and you may not have sent out very clear signals. You will need to weigh carefully each person's input and decide how useful and accurate the information is. If you find that all of the outside sources are in general agreement but it does not reflect your own perception, you will need to take a hard look in the mirror and adjust your personal perception as necessary.

I recommend evaluating at least three general areas.

Evaluate Where You Are in God's Training Process

In chapter 5 we discussed in detail God's training and equipping process for Christian leaders. A good place to begin a self-assessment is to map out your life up to the present and identify where you are in God's time line. What is your current stage of development? What tests and trials have you experienced and what have you learned from them? Particularly, what are the tests or trials you have yet to pass or are struggling with?

You will need to provide some basic background information to the people whom you ask to help you. Probably the easiest way to proceed is to copy chapter 6, which outlines God's training process, and have the people helping you read through this material before providing their input.

Evaluate Your Leadership and Behavioral Styles

In chapter 1 we described the basic leadership and behavioral styles that exist and identified some instruments you can use to assess your current styles. After taking the tests you are ready to answer a different series of questions for each.

LEADERSHIP STYLE

- What is your dominant leadership style?
- Do you change your style based on different leadership situations?
- Are you relying too heavily on the supporting style?
- Can you see the advantages of moving to more of a coaching style?
- Are you willing to try and change your leadership style?
- What changes would be necessary in your leadership style in order to make that change?

BEHAVIORAL STYLE

- What is your dominant behavioral style?
- What is your backup behavioral style, if there is one?

- As you read through the strengths and weaknesses of your present behavioral style, are there any elements that surprise you? Were you already aware of these strengths and weaknesses?
- Are you comfortable with your behavioral style? Do you try and change your behavioral style in certain situations because you feel your present behavioral style is not adequate?
- Can you see how God has used others like you in leadership situations?

For the individuals you have involved in your personal evaluation process, you will need either to purchase additional instruments and have them assess you using those instruments or provide the basic information given in earlier chapters and have them estimate where they see you on the various scales.

Evaluate Yourself Compared to Effective Coaches

In chapter 7 we listed and described in detail the major characteristics of successful coaches. Do a personal assessment for each characteristic and determine the degree to which you feel you currently exhibit this characteristic. Note in particular those items that you currently believe are weaknesses rather than strengths.

Again you should provide the necessary background information to those who are going to evaluate you. Devise some kind of scale or rating they can use to evaluate you on each of the characteristics.

Celebrate the Past

Self-analysis or self-evaluation can be painful as we begin to see areas that need to be changed. Since most of us seem to be more negatively focused anyway, it is not hard to see many areas that need to be changed.

But there is also a positive side to a personal assessment. We begin to see God's pattern or divine design in our lives. We see how we have grown and developed along the way. We see how much God has entrusted to us as well as the opportunities he has provided for us to learn and to lead. This should create a sense of joy and excitement.

We need to take time to stop and celebrate the past. All of your preparation has been for a reason, and you are well along the path of development. Maybe you need to go back and review the scriptural leadership principles discussed in chapter 5. You need to stand back and see the big picture rather than just focus on your current circumstances. Often current circumstances are so difficult that they cause us to lose focus and direction. We need to gain the proper perspective if we are going to be able to change.

Once you get the macro perspective, you should be able to celebrate even some of the things you originally saw as failures, because you can now see the lessons you have learned along the way. Some of our most dismal failures and painful experiences can become the greatest springboards to personal development. You need to celebrate the steps you have made toward Christian maturity and ministry fruitfulness. You need to thank God for his work in your life.

Creating a New Future

> Connecting with one's dreams releases one's passion, energy, and excitement about life. In leaders, such passion can arouse enthusiasm in those they lead. The key is uncovering your ideal self—the person you would like to be, including what you want in your life and work.[6]
>
> Daniel Goleman

> Where there is no revelation, the people cast off restraint.
>
> Proverbs 29:18

Once the self-analysis phase is complete, we move on to charting a new future. We decide where we are going and why. We redevelop our vision for the future. We capture or recapture God's perspective for our future.

This can start out as simply addressing the needs we discovered during the self-analysis. But it must also include a picture of what we believe God wants us to accomplish and what we will look like and be like as we accomplish his purposes for our lives. It is an attempt to see ourselves in the future as God sees us. We need to remove the limiting factors of today and by faith look to the future. What will that future look like? What will we be doing? What kind of a leader will we be?

What kinds of character traits will we have developed? What kinds of leadership skills will we exhibit?

This step requires a serious time of reflection. It cannot be done hurriedly, and it cannot be done while you are thinking and dealing with other issues. Normally you need to plan some significant time to be by yourself. You need to pray, dream, and begin to sketch out that future. The better that you can define that future in writing, the clearer the picture will be. It does not have to be long, but it must provide a picture that is both clear and compelling.

Making Change a Reality

> If you don't have a positive plan for your future, you may well be putting your relational and physical health at risk.[7]
>
> John Trent

The last phase in the change cycle is planning how you are going to move from where you are (what you discovered in the assessment phase) to where you want to go (what you discovered in the visioning phase). Leaders should not take a shotgun approach whereby they hope to hit something, but rather a rifle approach whereby they can clearly identify their targets. There are at least three key steps during this phase.

Developing Specific Objectives and Action Steps

You start by identifying specific objectives (targets) for what you want to accomplish. It is best to keep this list relatively short (five to seven objectives). Trying to do too much too fast can be discouraging, and you will quickly lose focus. Remember that change takes time. You must be careful not to set your objectives too high, too fast. It is not uncommon to set targets that are too optimistic for the first year. At this point you may need to consult with other key leaders to assess what it is you are trying to accomplish and give you the necessary feedback for setting reasonable objectives.

Once you have identified your objectives, you need to determine how you plan to accomplish each objective. What is it that you need to do to accomplish the objective? What specific action steps must you take? Again, if you are unable to decide how you should proceed, you may need to consult with key leaders around you who can give you some guidance and direction. There are several directions you can go with these action steps.

PERSONAL STUDY

One of the key elements you will want to consider is a personal study regimen that will move you toward your objectives. This should include a plan for studying key leaders in the Bible, particularly those who have a behavioral style similar to your own. It also should include identifying key books, tapes, and other resources, both Christian and secular, that you need to study in order to fulfill your objectives. You will need to develop a regular schedule that includes time for this personal study.

TRAINING OPPORTUNITIES

You may want to consider more formal training opportunities to meet your objectives. This might include attending specific seminars, visiting key churches, conducting interviews with key leaders, attending classes, or pursuing additional degrees. The key is that you are driving the agenda. You know what you need, and you are pursuing these opportunities that will best meet your personal objectives. You must be very selective as you decide what to include. You are no longer interested in just attending an event; rather, you are looking for specific outcomes.

Church Consultants Group is one company that offers a complete certification program to help train master coaches.[8]

Working Your Plan

Once you have identified your action steps, then the actual implementation phase begins. It is strongly recommended that as you carry out your plan, you develop a mentoring relationship with someone you trust and respect.

One of the real breakthroughs in the last several years is the rediscovery of the importance of mentors in a training process. As we mentioned in the discussion of leadership failure, most of us have not had the opportunity to be properly mentored. If we have, it has been by accident rather than by design. And yet we know from experience as well as from the Scriptures that proper mentoring is a key ingredient in leadership development.

Different kinds of mentoring relationships can be developed. But for purposes of personal growth, the best is one whereby you can develop an ongoing relationship with someone who is where you want to be in five to ten years. Ideally your mentor would be someone who has had to work through the key problems and issues that you will face and who can help guide you through the process. Again, this must be a very focused effort. If you can minister alongside your mentor, this is best. But if not, try to meet regularly with your mentor. You should go over your personal development plan with your mentor and chart the steps you want to take.

There are several aspects of personal development that can be enhanced through the use of a mentor:

- Maintaining and enhancing self-esteem
- Focusing on specific behavior, facts, and events
- Observing and assessing
- Diagnosing the environment
- Questioning
- Active and interactive listening
- Providing reinforcement[9]

Another key aspect of your implementation process must be significant times devoted to the practice of your new leadership skills. Isn't it interesting that great athletes spend most of their time practicing and very little time performing, while typical leaders spend virtually no time practicing and all of their time performing? Leadership skills are developed through both mental rehearsal and actual practice. These practice sessions allow for excellent feedback opportunities and the necessary adjustments as you grow and develop.

Evaluating Progress

As the old saying goes, "You don't get what you expect; you only get what you inspect." This simply means that a personal development plan must include personal accountability. You should use one or both of the following evaluation strategies.

EVALUATION AS PART OF YOUR MENTORING PROCESS

Your mentoring relationship provides an excellent opportunity for evaluation and accountability. We recommend that each mentoring session include at least three elements.

- Review of what has taken place since the previous meeting, including what progress has been made on your learning objectives.
- Discussion of key problems you have encountered where you need the advice and counsel from your mentor.
- Discussion of what you intend to accomplish between now and your next meeting with your mentor.

The mentor can provide a key point of accountability as well as a source of wisdom. In a genuine mentoring relationship, this accountability includes every area of your life. You must develop a transparency and openness with your mentor that allows for full revelation and interaction. A true mentor does not deal just with skill issues but also with character issues. Mentoring provides on-the-job training where you can work through the implementation of your desired changes. By submitting to such a mentoring process, you significantly increase the likelihood of accomplishing your learning objectives.

PERSONAL EVALUATION

It is possible to design your own evaluation process based on your needs. Generally speaking, there are two types of evaluation depending on the kind of objective you have set for yourself.

If you have an objective that is very measurable in nature, you may be able to evaluate it simply by defining various levels of success based on objective data. For example, you could define success by the number of pages of material that you've read, the number of seminars you've attended, and so forth. However, remember that objectives like these are just measuring the process, not necessarily the results of the process.

It is likely, however, that you will find many of your objectives are much more subjective in nature. How do you evaluate these? It's done all the time. You design a simple series of assessment questions that measure the qualities you are looking for and then have people you trust rate you on each item with some type of scale that you develop. By doing this regularly, you can clearly track progress.

Summary

Effective leaders grow and change because they want to and because they approach their personal growth in an intentional way. We can grow and change because of serendipitous events in our lives, but we cannot depend on that kind of learning as the foundation for a personal change process. We need to go through a planning cycle whereby we continually evaluate where we are, where we want to go, develop plans to get us there, and then evaluate our progress. This kind of active learning is much more likely to produce the desired changes. It is also much more likely to speed up the process. While it takes time, it is well worth the effort.

Questions for Reflection

1. Would it be helpful to include others in your self-evaluation? If so, whom should you choose?
2. Assuming you have identified some areas of leadership weakness or areas that you definitely would like to strengthen, what is your personal plan for changing your behavior in these areas? How will you move from where you are today to where you want to be in the future?
3. Are you currently involved in a formal mentoring process? If not, do you think it would increase your leadership effectiveness to develop one? If so, who would be the person (or persons) you should contact to see if he or she (or they) would be willing to serve as your mentor(s)?

9

DEALING WITH
EXTERNAL ISSUES
THAT INFLUENCE
LEADERSHIP
EFFECTIVENESS

- ■ MINISTRY FIT
- ■ VISION CASTING: DEFINING THE CHURCH'S STRATEGIC PLAN
- ■ SPIRITUAL GIFT DISCOVERY
- ■ THE ROLE OF OUTSIDE LEADERSHIP RESOURCES
- ■ THE ROLE OF MINISTRY TEAMS
- ■ ORGANIZATIONAL STRUCTURE
- ■ DECISION MAKING: VOTING
- ■ SUMMARY

While in the past we may have wanted loyal employees, today we need flexible people who are not possessive about "the way things are done around here."[1]

Spencer Johnson

Change begins when emotionally intelligent leaders actively question the emotional reality and the cultural norms underlying the group's daily activities and behavior. To create resonance—and results—the leader has to pay attention to the hidden dimensions: people's emotions, the undercurrents of the emotional reality in the organization, and the culture that holds it all together.[2]

Daniel Goleman

Y ou may remember our discussion in chapter 2 about why there is so much leadership failure in today's churches. Some of these issues relate to Christian leaders themselves, and in the last chapter we discussed how you can begin to address such issues. However, we also identified some issues that are external in nature and can seriously impair Christian leadership effectiveness. This chapter looks at these external issues and gives some guidelines for how you can deal with them.

If you don't deal consciously with these issues, you may find yourself in a situation where *you* are making the necessary personal changes but *your environment* is still hampering your leadership efforts. This is a more difficult area to work with because you don't have the level of control over this area that you do with personal issues. In this chapter we will deal with some of the most important elements of the ministry environment.

Ministry Fit

Every church functions in a unique context. Understanding the context and its implications is particularly important for Christian leaders. The level of church health and effectiveness is directly related to the degree of ministry fit. Churches that have a high degree of ministry fit normally have significantly more health and effectiveness. Churches that have a low degree of ministry fit normally experience more conflict and diminished effectiveness. Ministry fit is based on three primary variables.

- *Ministry Area Profile.* The specific geographical context of a local church is a significant variable for ministry fit. Churches can generally assume that their ministry area is defined by an average drive time of fifteen to twenty minutes. There are ex-

ceptions where geographical or psychological barriers change
the boundaries of the ministry area, but generally speaking most
people are not going to drive more than fifteen to twenty minutes
to attend a church.

The demographic characteristics (age, income, ethnicity, education, and so on) of a church's ministry area affect its opportunity
for ministry and community impact. Equally important are the
psychographic characteristics (beliefs, opinions, attitudes). Taken
together, these characteristics define the kind of people that
live in the church's ministry area. It is essential that the church
understand these characteristics and their implications because
they will have a profound effect upon the church's ministry.

- *Congregational Profile.* The second major variable related to
  ministry fit is the congregational profile. This refers to the demographic and psychographic characteristics of those who are part of
  the church family. Every church is able to attract and keep people
  with certain demographic and psychographic characteristics, but
  not others. The makeup of the congregation is a very important
  variable relative to ministry fit. Who is or who is not already in
  the church determines to a large degree the kind of people the
  church can attract and keep. Understanding the congregational
  profile also means understanding the culture that has developed
  in the church. What are the key elements of church life that are
  highly valued by the constituents? Equally important is what elements are held in low esteem. Interestingly, visitors to churches
  are able to pick up signals immediately that help them understand
  the unique culture of each church.

- *Pastoral Profile.* Because of the significant role senior pastors
  play in the life of the church, they become the third key variable
  related to ministry fit. It is important that the pastor himself as
  well as the church leaders understand the implications of the
  demographic and psychographic makeup of the senior pastor as
  well as the unique vision that God has placed in his heart. These
  characteristics significantly affect the ability of the church to reach
  different kinds of people in its ministry area. Generally speaking,
  people are attracted to a church where the profile and vision of
  the senior pastor either is like theirs or is at least compatible.

The degree to which these three variables overlap is the degree to
which there is a ministry fit. When the three profiles are very similar,

there is a good ministry fit, and generally healthy and effective ministry follows. When the three profiles are dissimilar, the opposite is normally true. Let's look at some of the possibilities, particularly where there is poor ministry fit.

- *Virtually no overlap between the ministry area profile, the congregational profile, and the pastoral profile.* This is the worst-case scenario. A congregation has a pastor who does not fit with the congregation, and the church is trying to do ministry in an area that does not fit with either its own profile or the profile of its pastor. As you can well imagine, the opportunity for effective ministry is minimal. Something has to change for the church to increase its ministry fit.
- *The pastoral profile and the ministry area profile are similar, but the congregational profile is dissimilar.* This happens more often than people might realize. Unfortunately, it creates a lot of tension in the church. The pastor is able to attract people from the community, but they do not fit well with the existing congregation. If the growth is rapid, it is possible that the new people will become the dominant faction in the congregation. This usually results in significant numbers of people leaving the church during the transition. The more likely scenario is slow growth with the new people finding it very difficult to assimilate into the congregation and eventually leaving the church to find a better fit somewhere else.
- *The pastoral profile and the congregational profile are similar, but the ministry area profile is dissimilar.* This is also a common pattern. The church hires a pastor that fits their profile, or the pastor develops a congregation that fits his profile; however, neither is a good match with the ministry area. This means a limited opportunity for the church to expand its ministry.
- *The congregational profile and the ministry area profile are similar, but the pastoral profile is dissimilar.* This scenario, which is the least likely of the four, usually leads to a pastoral change after a few years.

As you can see from these scenarios, it is important for pastors and church leaders to understand the demographic and psychographic dynamics that are affecting the life of the congregation. If the church wants to have maximum impact in its ministry area, the pastor and the church leaders must figure out ways to increase ministry fit. This can

be done but must be faced openly and honestly by the entire church
leadership team if real change is going to take place.

Vision Casting: Defining the Church's Strategic Plan

> Regardless of the stress of circumstance, institutions function better
> when the idea, the dream, is to the fore, and the person, the leader,
> is seen as servant of the idea.[3]
>
> Robert K. Greenleaf

A second way to shape your ministry environment and at the same
time provide yourself with a significant opportunity to lead is in your
role as vision caster. The area in which you can and should most influence the direction of the church is in helping to define the mission and
vision of the church or your area of ministry. It is essential that a church
have a strategic plan that fits its unique context and composition. Two
primary factors explain why defining the mission and vision (strategic
plan) are so important: (1) the limited resources in the church, and
(2) the need to reduce the number of competing agendas operating
within the church.

If churches had unlimited funds, facilities, and volunteers, clarifying
the focus of the church and its ministries might not be so important, but
since these are limited in every church, it becomes necessary to define
the mission and vision so these precious resources are not wasted.

The issue of competing agendas is also a serious problem. If a church
has not taken the time to define clearly where it is going and what
it will look like, everyone who is part of the congregation or ministry
is forced to try and define it for themselves. The primary place most
people start is with what they personally *want* or *need*. The result is a
shopping-list approach to ministry that never satisfies and is bound to
produce controversy. Where this normally surfaces is in the church's
budgeting process or during attempts to change the church's organizational structure. Who gets how much and who gains or loses power
become the criteria for people to guess the direction of the church.
Power and control replace mission and vision as the controlling elements of the church or ministry.

As we have defined earlier, one of the key roles a Christian leader
must fulfill is in setting both the tone and the direction of the church
or ministry. The best way you can do this is through the development
of a clear and compelling strategic plan.

I believe that the mission and vision of the church or ministry (what I would call a strategic plan) should include the following elements:

Church Culture/Personality

> Every church is driven by something. There is a guiding force, a controlling assumption, a directing conviction behind everything that happens. It may be unspoken. It may be unknown to many. But it is there, influencing every aspect of the church's life. . . . Growing, healthy churches have a clear cut identity. They understand their reason for being; they are precise in their purpose. They know exactly what God has called them to do. They know what their business is, and they know what is none of their business.
>
> Rick Warren

Every church has a somewhat unique culture or personality. As a consultant I usually discover that the church is unaware of its own culture or personality, and what has developed was not done intentionally. Over time, as a result of the ministry leadership in the church and the people it attracted, the culture has evolved. People in the church are often surprised to find out that visitors to the church quickly identify the culture or personality of the church and are surprisingly accurate. It only makes sense that every church or ministry needs to be much more intentional in defining God's desired culture or personality for their future. Culture or personality involves several aspects.

VALUES

Values are the things we believe about the ministry that are non-negotiable. Values are the foundational principles upon which you intend to develop your ministry. Values reflect how you want things to be, not necessarily how they are now.

DISTINCTIVES

Distinctives can be defined as (1) unusual or unique attributes of the church or ministry as it sees itself in the future, (2) unusual or unique attributes that make it different from other churches or other ministries, and (3) special things God seems to be doing or wants to do. This is seen in the gifts, talents, and abilities of those God has placed in the congregation or ministry. It is also seen in the special burdens or concerns of the people involved. A distinctive must be something that is believed or demonstrated by a significant number of leaders and constituents.

An assumption can be defined as (1) a belief or a conviction that is taken for granted about the way things ought to be, (2) a claim and presumption supported by either individuals or groups but may not be able to be proved objectively, (3) a perception of facts that are held as truth until they are effectively challenged, and (4) a thing we believe is true or should be true that helps define and prioritize our values. Assumptions help define who we are.

Mission Statement

I define "mission" as "the biblical mandate for every church or ministry regardless of context." Mission focuses on the basic priorities and principles given for all churches in the New Testament. This means determining the general outline and shape of ministry for the church, what some would call a "purpose-driven" church. While the labels may differ from church to church, most churches would agree that the mission of the church includes the Great Commission (Matt. 18:19–20; Mark 16:15–16; Luke 24:47–48; Acts 1:8) and the great commandments (Matt. 22:37–40).

Translated into the terminology of most churches, mission would include the following elements, although they might be grouped differently.[4]

1. Assimilation
   - Small group ministry
   - Visitor follow-up
   - New member classes/orientation
2. Discipleship/Spiritual Growth
   - Christian education classes
   - Spiritual disciplines
   - Mentoring
3. Evangelism/Outreach
   - Evangelism training
   - Evangelistic events/activities

4. Missions
- Local, national, and international missions
- Benevolence for those in need outside the church
- Church planting

5. Pastoral Care
- Short-term counseling
- Crisis care/counseling
- Benevolence for those in need inside the church
- Recovery groups

6. Training and Equipping
- Spiritual gifts discovery
- Volunteer involvement
- Ministry training

7. Worship
- Drama
- Music
- Celebrative arts

The labels or titles may be different from church to church, but these form the foundational elements of the church's mission.

Vision Statement

Vision defines where the church or ministry is going and what it will look like and feel like in the future. It gives everybody advance notice of what the church or ministry will and will not do, what the church or ministry will and will not look like. I define vision as the following: **a compelling and enduring picture of God's preferred future for us—what God wants us to look like and be like as we fulfill his mission in our unique context.**

The development of a clear vision statement allows constituents to choose whether or not they want to support and participate in the fulfillment of the vision. This is particularly important in our mobile society where people move easily from church to church or ministry to ministry. If the constituents feel the vision is contrary to where they want to go, after they hear the church's vision is a good time for them to move on to another place where their personal vision is more compatible.

- The future we are talking about is not a composition of what we want individually for the future but what we believe *God* wants for our future. It therefore means putting aside our personal agendas as much as possible. It's okay to recognize what those agendas might be, but the attempt is to keep those from interfering with the visioning process.
- The future we are talking about is not just an improved version of our past. While God has obviously been laying a foundation for the future in the present ministry, we should not automatically assume that our future will look like either the past or the present. We need to keep our minds and hearts open to what God wants to do, which could mean a significant amount of change for our future. If the history of the early church is any indication of what our future might look like, we are all in for more than a few surprises.

Few churches or ministries have taken the time to define such a vision statement, although parachurch ministries generally do a better job of clearly defining who they are and what they are setting out to do. If a church or ministry has a genuine vision statement, two things should be clear from that statement.

- What things will you do that most churches or ministries would never or seldom do?
- What things will you seldom or never do that most churches or ministries would normally do?

If you cannot answer these questions, you do not have a unique vision statement that will guide you in the future.

Vision Implications

A list of implications from the vision statement is critical for understanding what the vision statement will mean for the future. Even churches or ministries that have done a great job of writing a vision statement often neglect this step because they assume everyone knows the implications that logically follow from the vision statement. However, the average person definitely does not know the answers and needs the implications clarified so they can understand the direction.

The implications help to explain what changes will need to take place in order to fulfill the vision. This is particularly important as you plan for the future.

There are many ways that a church or ministry can determine its strategic plan, including getting significant input from key constituents. But ultimately it is the job of the pastoral staff, board, and key lay leaders to come up with the actual plan. It is expected that the senior pastor or ministry head will initiate the process and lead others to a strategic plan that represents a significant consensus on the part of the leadership team. How the church determines its strategic plan says a lot about what it believes about leadership as well as about what it values.

Leading in the establishment of a strategic plan is a unique opportunity for Christian leaders to create a positive ministry environment in which they can flourish. By providing a key leadership role in the strategic planning process, Christian leaders enhance their opportunity to lead and reduce the power and control of those who oppose them.

Spiritual Gift Discovery

A third way pastors and ministry leaders can significantly improve their ministry environment is getting more people involved in ministry and getting them ministering in the right places. When people are actively involved and using their spiritual gifts, they are more committed to the church in every way and in most cases are much more respectful of genuine Christian leadership.

Over the last ten years there has been a lot of discussion and ministry planning around the concept of spiritual gift discovery. The basic concept behind this effort is that all Christians have spiritual gifts and that as we help people discover their gifts, they will be more productive and fulfilled as they carry out ministries using these gifts. However, the various programs that have been created to make this happen have not been particularly successful. Some of the major problems have been as follows:

- Constituents basically view these programs as a new way to fill needed slots in the church volunteer workforce and therefore avoid the discovery programs. Very few churches do include ministry opportunities at the end that go beyond the walls of the church, and even fewer match gifts to parachurch ministries operating beyond the local church.

- By far the majority of the programs use some form of self-discovery process for identifying spiritual gifts. The accuracy of these results can vary significantly depending on the spiritual maturity and experience of the person taking the tests. It appears that in the early church spiritual gift discovery was much more a function of the leaders, including commissioning or ordination for the leadership gifts. Very few ministry leaders today see this as one of their functions.

- Churches have failed to identify which volunteer positions are related to which spiritual gifts and which positions are simply chores that need to be done in order for the church to function. Husbands and wives do not debate who has the spiritual gift of taking out the garbage or changing diapers. These jobs are decided by mutual consent with a realization that they are jobs that must be done, regardless of the talent, temperament, or gifts of the individuals involved. The same must be true in the church.

- People go through the initial stages of the training to discover their gifts but drop out before they are ever implemented into ministry because of fear of getting trapped into a volunteer position in the church.

- Churches have a tough time matching up spiritual gifts with all of the jobs and volunteer ministries in the church. Thus, even if people go through all the training, it is still not clear where they should go next.

Christian leaders will need to decide what they are going to do to help people discover and use their spiritual gifts. The concept is biblical, but the execution to this point has been questionable. It is not a matter of if but how.

The Role of Outside Leadership Resources

The fourth way pastors and ministry leaders can significantly improve their ministry environment is in developing the necessary relationships with outside leadership resources. Ephesians 4 speaks of apostles, prophets, evangelists, pastors, and teachers. While the first three of these are primarily leaders who had ministry responsibilities beyond the scope of the local church, pastors and teachers were primarily leaders at the local church level. In the early church these leaders, who were identified as a gift to the church, played significant roles in the ministry of local congregations.

The underlying issue here is the degree to which the church is going to depend only on its own internal leadership resources. In many ways the rise of denominations somewhat replaced the roles provided in the first century by the apostles, prophets, and evangelists. However, with the declining influence of denominations, pastors often look to leadership resources outside the church for wisdom and guidance.

Several different resources for Christian leadership have developed outside the local church. One has been the emergence of new pastoral associations and networks where pastors can get encouragement and guidance. Some of these are geographically oriented, some center on the ministry of successful megachurches, others focus on churches with similar ministry styles. A second outside leadership resource that has flourished in the last twenty-five years has been the development of parachurch ministries. They generally specialize in one aspect of ministry but have become an outstanding source of expertise beyond the borders of the local church. A third resource that we discussed in the last chapter has been the reemergence of mentoring relationships where one pastor tutors another. And finally, there has been the reemergence in some church circles of the fivefold ministry described in Ephesians 4.

All of these resources are available to assist the local church in developing its own ministry. Each church has to decide how it will relate to these Christian leaders outside of their own local church environment. There are two obvious choices.

- The church may decide it has more than enough internal leadership resources. Therefore, while the pastor may involve himself in denominational meetings or other types of networking, as far as the local church is concerned the only real training or encouragement for leaders will be through internal leadership resources (pastor, elders, board, and so on).
- The church may decide it does not by God's design have all of the necessary leadership resources that are necessary and therefore should be open to instruction, guidance, counsel, and exhortation from leaders outside the local church. Once this decision is

made, the question becomes which outside leadership resources the church will use.

Most pastors, ministry leaders, and churches have decided the second approach makes most sense. However, the development of relationships with these outside resources has not been very intentional. Very little thought has been given to which resources should be used and why. The rise of denominational leadership provided a simple and fixed answer, but the results varied significantly from church to church.

Obviously working with any outside resource implies that the local church must know and trust these outside leaders. This kind of relationship requires significant time and effort on the part of both parties. This was also true in the first century. The relationship between local church leaders and those with more itinerant ministries was significant. It was not based so much on authority as it was on relationship.

Because churches today are much freer to develop whatever relationships they desire, the thinking has come full circle. Now many churches are rethinking the early church model. Regardless of which outside resources the church chooses to work with, it is obvious that there needs to be a lot of thought and planning if the church is going to see the desired result. This in itself provides another excellent opportunity for pastors and ministry leaders to provide the necessary intentional leadership model for which God designed them.

The Role of Ministry Teams

The fifth vital area in which Christian leaders can establish a positive ministry environment is in their working relationship with their ministry team. This includes such bodies as councils and boards. Every church or ministry has some kind of leadership team that provides general oversight. Because clarity has been lacking when it comes to the role and function of these leadership teams, the members assume they are a miniature version of either the U.S. Supreme Court or the U.S. Congress. Both are inaccurate analogies for the kind of team leadership expected in New Testament ministry. The result is micromanagement on the part of the leadership team and an adversarial relationship with pastors, staff, and ministry leaders. Most leadership teams view their role as making sure the leaders (the executive branch) do not misuse their power and therefore see their function as watchdogs, guarding the congregation or ministry from executive abuse.

Based on the early church model that was described in chapter 3, it seems best for the church to have one leadership team that includes all the leaders (pastors, elders, and so forth) who are responsible for the oversight of the church or ministry. This provides unity and the necessary support to carry out the ministry.

Fortunately, there is some new thinking in regard to how nonprofit boards can and should function (including churches), which is helpful. John Carver's "Policy Governance" is one of the best models in use today for understanding how nonprofit boards can operate. His book *Boards That Make a Difference* (San Francisco: Jossey-Bass, 1997) provides clear thoughts and specific recommendations for nonprofit boards, particularly those that focus on administrative oversight. His work also applies to ministry leadership, including councils or ministry teams.

Carver's work with NPOs (nonprofit organizations) and organizations in general has led to a flexible model that can be adopted by and adapted to nearly any institution. The following is not intended to be a comprehensive teaching on "Policy Governance" but an introduction to some fundamental principles put forth by Carver:

- The board represents the ownership of the organization just as a business board represents its stockholders.
- The power of boards is not as individuals but as a group, a corporate entity entrusted with the authority to govern and lead the organization.
- Policy Governance requires boards to deliberate and write down their most significant policies and to do so in a carefully crafted way. The board of directors must address the largest or broadest policies in four categories in order to fulfill this mandate.

    — *Organizational Outcomes.* The board defines which results are to be achieved, for whom, and at what cost.

    — *Executive Limitations.* The board establishes the boundaries of acceptability within which leaders can operate.

    — *Board-Executive Relationship.* The board clarifies the manner in which it delegates authority to staff as well as how it evaluates performance based on provisions of the Organizational Outcomes as well as the Executive Limitations policies.

    — *Board Process.* The board determines its philosophy, its accountability, and the specifics of its own job.

- The board takes the responsibility for defining policies and then delegates the responsibility for the fulfillment of those policies to the leaders.
- The board, led by the pastors and staff, develops a clear strategic plan. This includes defining the mission, vision, and culture (assumptions, values, and distinctives) of the organization. In its ultimate simplicity, the strategic plan defines what, how, for whom, and at what cost.
- The distinction between strategic planning and means enables the board to free itself from trivia, to delegate clearly and powerfully, and to turn its attention to the larger issues that provide the necessary direction for the church.
- The board defines how it will work with the pastors and staff as well as how it will monitor the performance of the senior pastor. By establishing the parameters ahead of time, there is less likelihood that the board or the pastors and staff will operate in each other's sphere of responsibility.
- The board must define its own operation. This includes clearly defining roles and responsibilities of individual members, board officers, board committees, and the board as a whole.
- Accountability is a genuine and necessary part of organizational success. However, the criteria must be clearly established and relate directly to the factors that best determine organizational success. In this model the core of the senior pastor evaluation centers on Organizational Outcomes and Executive Limitation policies.

The only area where I disagree with Carver is on how the strategic plan is to be produced. Carver believes that it should be the role of the board to produce that plan with *input* from the senior pastor, staff, or ministry leader. This I believe is a violation of the leadership principles discussed throughout this book. In a church setting, if the church board were constituted with the idea that every board member was a pastor/elder and every pastor/elder was a board member, I wouldn't be as concerned with this format. However, I still believe that the senior pastor (as the "first among equals") should demonstrate leadership by initiating the process and providing the initial ideas.

But in situations where the board is composed of only "administrative" elders or deacons, and the pastors are carrying out the actual ministry of the church, to ask the board to formulate the mission and vision would be a big mistake.

The same holds true for staff and ministry leaders. I have encountered numerous examples in my consulting experience where a staff member or ministry leader is required to report to multiple boards or individuals who have no direct involvement or commitment to that area of ministry. The result is confusion for everyone involved.

Another excellent resource for church governance is *Elders and Leaders* by Gene Getz.[5] This is an outstanding book that raises all the right questions in a thorough study of the Scriptures. It then explains the actual decisions Getz's church made regarding these questions. This would be a good book for elders or board/council members to read through together and discuss, both the concepts and the implications for their own church.

Organizational Structure

> The assumption here is that if an institution is well led, the nature of the formal structure is much less important than if it is poorly led. If the leadership is exceptionally good, an institution sometimes operates without much reference to formal structure, even though it may have a well-defined one.[6]
>
> Robert K. Greenleaf

Most pastors or ministry leaders would point to the organizational structure as their biggest impediment to leadership and would want to start there in making changes. I do not recommend this strategy. Changes to the organizational structure usually take a long time, are very contentious, and require difficult voting requirements.

While it is true that the organizational structure can significantly impact the ability of Christian leaders to lead, it is better to focus first on other areas such as the ones mentioned earlier in this chapter. If you start there, you have a much greater opportunity to enhance your leadership credibility and the overall effectiveness of the organization.

While there is significant freedom in how a church can design its organizational structure, certain principles are critical if Christian leadership is to prevail. Basically, U.S. churches are organized around one of three governing principles:

- Congregational—Emphasizes congregational leadership, democratic format.
- Presbyterian—Emphasizes board or elder leadership.
- Episcopal—Emphasizes pastoral or staff leadership.

What I have tried to argue for in this book is a combination of the three systems, as follows:

- Congregational in the sense that congregational members have significant opportunity to give ministry input, and ministry leaders (whether staff or lay leaders) have the freedom to lead and carry out their ministries as long as they are fulfilling the mission and vision of the church.
- Presbyterian in the sense that elders, staff, or board members form a leadership team or leadership community in which the mission and vision of the church or ministry is defined and accountability is maintained.
- Episcopal in the sense that pastors and ministry leaders as "firsts among equals" have the responsibility to provide significant leadership within the leadership team.

You need to evaluate your current organizational structure to determine its current and future effectiveness. Some churches are limited by denominational rules in terms of what the organizational structure can look like and how it must function. Others have more freedom in this area. If you are limited by denominational rules, you must decide how you can best function within the present system. It is interesting that in congregational surveys church constituents often say they do not believe the present organizational structure of the church is the best for facilitating the ministry in the church itself. They have observed the incredible waste of human resources, the conflict that emerges, and they want something better.

Decision Making: Voting

As previously discussed, voting is a much overused concept in the decision-making processes of churches today. You simply cannot make a strong case for voting in the New Testament, even among the leadership team, and certainly not on the part of the congregation as a whole. While it may be allowed, it should not be the primary way to make decisions. If the church requires that every decision be voted upon, you can see why the church is forced to become a political arena that is focused on itself rather than on its mission and vision.

What many church leaders interpret as a demand from members of the congregation to vote on issues is really nothing more than people wanting to have a significant say. They want their opinions to be heard, and they see some form of vote as the only way this can happen. Churches that work hard in the area of communication have learned that usually voting is not the issue.

That being said, since voting has been institutionalized in most churches and in most cases has been written into the bylaws of the church, it is very difficult to change. If the church has had a history of congregational government, or if significant numbers of people in the congregation have come from churches with a congregational form of government, trying to transition to another format may prove difficult. That is why I discussed this issue last. It is the most difficult to change and has the greatest potential for conflict of any of the issues previously discussed. It should not be attempted until the leadership team (pastor, elders, board) has a significant consensus on the issue and is willing to spend the time and effort necessary to effect the change.

One area where gradual change can be made is in the decision making done at the top level of church leadership. Decision making at the leadership level generally should be done by consensus. This allows for open debate and discussion but is not as divisive as the casting of ballots. Just as many churches have moved away from a formal use of Robert's "Rules of Order," they also can adjust the way they make decisions and move whenever possible away from using voting for decision making.

Summary

In this chapter I have tried to provide some ways whereby Christian leaders can improve their leadership environment, which is a key factor in their personal success. Most of us inherit our ministry environment and don't have the luxury of designing it at its inception, so we need to face the environmental issues just as much as we need to address our own personal leadership limitations. It only makes sense that we address the personal issues first and then begin making the necessary environmental changes. Sometimes simply making the personal changes is enough to change the ministry environment, but normally it must be done with intention and over a long period of time.

As discussed in several places in this chapter, changing the ministry environment takes a lot of hard work. In some cases the ministry environment is so toxic that effective Christian leaders discover that the only way they can pursue God's plan for them is to go to a different ministry setting. Good leaders who operate in severely dysfunctional organizations are either driven out or forced to succumb to the prevailing culture. A study of pastoral tenure, however, suggests that most pastors leave way too early in the process. The most effective years of ministry most often do not occur until the sixth to tenth years in a given ministry setting. Moving to a new ministry environment every four to six years will pretty much guarantee personal as well as ministry failure.

Questions for Reflection

1. What degree of ministry fit currently exists in your church? What are the implications?
2. Does your church have a vision for its future (a clear and compelling picture of God's future for the church)? If not, should one be developed? How?
3. What are you currently doing in your church to help people identify and use their spiritual gifts? Is it working? If not, what changes should you make to improve the process?
4. Which outside leadership resources, if any, do you believe you need to develop to enhance the ministry of your church? What do you need to do to develop or enhance these relationships?
5. Is your current church board working as effectively as it should? If not, what should you do to increase the effectiveness of the board?
6. How would you describe the current organizational structure of your church? Does it facilitate effective ministry or hinder it? What are the implications for the future?
7. How much does your church currently rely on voting for decision making? Do you feel that is the right balance, based on your understanding of Scripture? Should you consider changes in your decision-making processes in the church? If so, what changes should be targeted first?

10

LEADING IN DIFFICULT
TIMES

- MOVING FROM STRATEGY TO TACTICS
- FAILING TO UNDERSTAND WHY AND
  HOW CHRISTIAN LEADERS FAIL
- SUMMARY

We are all failures—at least, all the best of us are.[1]

J. M. Barrie

Let us not become weary in doing good, for at the proper time we
will reap a harvest if we do not give up.

Galatians 6:9

Success is never final; failure is never fatal.[2]

Joe Paterno

Dave had just finished his family vacation after a difficult year of
ministry in his church. Actually there had been many different
problems over the last several years. None seemed to be devastating,
but the sum of all of them had taken a big toll on the leaders of the
church, particularly Dave. As he began preparing to go back to work,
a terrible realization began to form in his mind: "I really have no desire
to go back to work in the church. In fact, just thinking about it takes
all of the joy and energy out of my life. What do I do now?" Dave began

to try and figure out the source of his confusion and discontent. However, the more he thought about it, the more he became depressed. Dave had worked in a business before he went into the pastorate, so he understood the need for planning, and he had led the church through several planning efforts. But it seemed like most of the plans failed or had very little effect on the health and effectiveness of the church. The thought of trying one more major planning effort was demoralizing to Dave.

Dave's experience is not atypical. Unfortunately, many pastors feel the way Dave did. Most want to continue pastoring and to find a way around the obstacles but wonder where they should begin. It seems like no matter what they try, the results are discouraging. In my experience as a consultant the problems stem from one of two major issues.

- *Inability to move from strategy to tactics.* This is the simplest issue but confuses many church leaders.
- *Failure to understand how and why Christian leaders fail.* This is a much more complex and difficult issue but is common in ministry.

Moving from Strategy to Tactics

Many people think of leadership as a single, constant dimension. However, there are several cycles or phases all leaders must go through. Perhaps the easiest is the planning phase. The reason this phase is the easiest is because it can be done in a relatively relaxed environment that does not require change. Planning can be done based on certain basic assumptions. The result of the planning phase is usually termed "strategy." That is, as a result of the planning, a strategy or series of strategies is established that the leader believes will best accomplish the task at hand.

The implementation phase, however, is much more difficult. This is where "strategy" must change to "tactics." Now the leader is faced with a continually changing environment, and constant adjustments must be made to the strategies. In some extreme cases the earlier strategies must be discarded entirely. All leaders must learn the basic skills of both strategy and tactics, but most will find they prefer one phase or the other. Some leaders seem to thrive in determining strategy, while others seem to do best when faced with changing circumstances.

It's much like a football team that plans and practices all week in preparation for a big game. What they have done up to kickoff is really strategic thinking. They have analyzed what they think their opponents will do. They have assessed what they think they can do. And they have come up with a game plan that they believe has the best chance for success. Most of this work is theoretical. We believe this, we assume this, therefore we should do that. It's hard work to do that kind of strategic thinking, and it is essential that it be done in preparation for the actual implementation phase.

The implementation phase is similar to what happens after kickoff. Now all the theory and strategy that have been developed during the week get tested in the reality of a game. The focus shifts from *strategy* to *tactics*. Tactics refers to the give-and-take that happens during the game. What if the opponent does something we didn't expect? What if some of our key players are unable to play? How should that change our strategy? What if our strategy isn't working? What adjustments are needed along the way?

Let's face it, nothing ever goes exactly as we plan. There are always things that surprise us, some of them good, some of them bad. Yet many pastors and ministry leaders operate as if this tactical side of planning never existed. How often have we seen a ministry outlive its usefulness and yet be continued? How often have we seen major changes in the composition or needs of the community, or the congregation, and yet the church operates as if nothing has changed. Change is a reality that churches must deal with. It was a problem for the first-century church, and it will continue to be a problem until the Lord comes. We are called to face it, not ignore it.

The Council of Jerusalem was a critical point in time for the church (see Acts 15). The church had to decide what rules and regulations it would impose on the new Gentile believers. Many of those who had a Jewish background wanted to see the same rules and traditions that belonged to their own past be part of the requirements for the new Gentile believers.

Under the wise leadership of the Holy Spirit, however, the apostles and the leaders of the church decided that the Gentile believers could function somewhat differently and yet be fully Christian. This decision laid the foundation for an incredible expansion of the church into the Gentile world. While this was a difficult transition for most people, including the apostle Peter, the church was able to adjust to the changing conditions, and as a result there was great fruitfulness.

Pastors and ministry leaders today must do the same rather than say, "We never did it that way before" or "We've always done it that way." They must be very serious about the leadership responsibilities given to them by God and do everything in their power to make sure the dreams become realities. This requires both willingness and commitment to change along the way.

Pastors and ministry leaders must regularly measure and assess their progress and then make the necessary adjustments or midcourse corrections. These should be viewed as normal. Assessment is a weak area in most churches. Few evaluate what they are doing in any kind of systematic way. Why?

- Fear of finding out that they are not achieving what they set out to do.
- Not wanting to get into a typical evaluation process that becomes interrogative and punitive.

Evaluation does not have to be a negative process. It's a necessary part of every area of our lives. Because some have had a negative experience with evaluation in school or on the job, they shy away from any type of evaluation in the church. However, the reason for assessment is to find out how you are doing and what you need to do to better meet the desired results. It should be a team approach, where the evaluator(s) and those being evaluated join together to ask hard questions about how they are progressing.

The solution when things are off track is to make the necessary adjustments. Maybe the strategy needs additional resources to succeed. If this is the case, the leadership team will have to decide if they can allocate the needed resources. If they can't, obviously expectations need to be lowered. In fact, the strategy may have to be scrapped if the necessary resources are simply not available. This does not imply that those attempting to carry out the strategy were at fault, but it does force both the leaders and the implementers to take a hard look at what they are doing and decide what adjustments need to be made.

Remember that strategies are the easiest thing to change. If the strategies selected by the team do not work as well as desired, they can be changed, or they can be eliminated and new strategies can be created that will have a better chance of accomplishing the desired task. Successful implementation demands flexibility and above all a results-oriented focus. The purpose of all the planning done by leaders is to accomplish specific ends. Whatever plans or strategies best meet this test are the ones leaders are looking for.

Good leaders don't worry about failure. Failure simply tells them one more plan or strategy that doesn't work. By constantly modifying and adapting their plans or strategies, they will get closer and closer to what they set out to accomplish.

The implementation phase is the real test of the leader's planning efforts. The intent from the beginning was to do the work of the ministry, not just talk about it. The goal was to be more focused, intentional, and proactive so that the leader and team could effectively carry out the assignment entrusted to them by God. The goal was not to be successful in a worldly sense, nor to boast about individual accomplishments, but simply to be good stewards or managers of everything God entrusted to the leader and the team.

Many pastors and ministry leaders are constantly trying to find an environment that doesn't require significant change, that remains relatively stable, that does not require difficult leadership. Unfortunately, that is a dream world. If anyone was faced by difficult times and the tyranny of the urgent, it was Jesus Christ. And yet, as J. Oswald Sanders points out, Jesus was able to provide all the leadership necessary without the treadmill mentality many today have in ministry.

> The secret of his serenity lay in his assurance that he was working according to his father's plan, a plan that embraced every hour, made provisions for every contingency. His calendar had been arranged and through communion with his father he received both each day the words he was supposed to say, and the works he was supposed to do.[3]

Failing to Understand Why and How Christian Leaders Fail

George Barna and George Gallup are noted researchers who have spent considerable time studying the attitudes and actions of Christians. As a result of their research, both have come to the disturbing conclusion that there is little noticeable difference between the attitudes and actions of non-Christians and "born-again believers."

Dallas Willard, a noted Christian writer, addressed the same question in his recent book *The Divine Conspiracy.*

> The most telling thing about the contemporary Christian is that he or she simply has no compelling sense that understanding and conformity with the clear teachings of Christ is of any vital importance to his or her life, and certainly not that it is any way essential.[4]

Willard adds the following comment:

> True, you will find few scholars or leaders in Christian circles who deny that we are supposed to make disciples or apprentices to Jesus and teach them to do all things that Jesus said. . . . Jesus' instructions on this matter are, after all, starkly clear. We just don't do what he said. We don't seriously attempt it. And apparently we don't know how to do it.[5]

As a church consultant I can certainly testify that a lot of what I have seen and heard, even at the highest levels of ministry leadership, has shocked me. It reminds me of a comment I heard years ago. Someone told me that if you study the Bible's major characters as well as Christian leaders throughout history, "few finish well." This has both shocked and inspired me.

When we become Christians, we are saying we want to become lifetime disciples of Christ. But the question is why so many Christ followers, including Christian leaders, choose to deviate from this plan?

The Great Disconnect

We are all disciples. The question is whose?

We all have learned from other people. Their influence has made us what we are. It's hard to come to terms with all this. Today, especially in Western cultures, we prefer to think, "I am my own person." We make up our own minds. But the reality is that to a great degree we are a product of those people who have had a significant influence in our lives. In our early lives we have little opportunity to decide our environment, and therefore the people in our sphere of influence may have provided positive or negative direction.

As we grow older we have more selection over those with whom we associate and therefore by whom we are influenced. When we become Christians, we naturally gravitate toward the church and other Christians for direction and influence. Unfortunately, most of our church "discipleship" programs are failures.

Most of what we call discipleship is simply giving people information about what Jesus believed, taught, and practiced. It's not doing what Jesus did or thinking like Jesus thought. We don't promise people that as a result of taking this class, they actually will act differently. If we take a class on learning to drive a car, wouldn't we expect to be able to drive a car at the end of the class? Or would we just expect to know how it's done?

The most significant problem is not with the church's training, however, but with how we learn to view Jesus Christ. If we were going to hold a party and could invite anyone we wanted, whom would we invite? Unfortunately, one of the last people we would think to invite would be Jesus. Why? Because we think of Jesus as judgmental. We think of him as someone who probably wouldn't add much in terms of personality. We certainly don't think of Jesus as a joyful person. In fact, the majority of us think of him as sort of morose.

If that is our view of Jesus, why would we want to be his disciples? Why would our love and devotion for him drive us to model our thoughts and actions after him? The fact is it wouldn't, and it doesn't.

Many of us can think back to our dating experiences with our spouse. We could not spend enough time together. And when we weren't together, we spent a great deal of time thinking of that person. This is the normal product of love. This is how we should be in our relationship with Jesus Christ.

Another major disconnect takes place when Christian leaders begin to act on their own and forget that their only real source of spiritual power and authority is God. Some of these leaders disconnect after they experience significant success and begin to "believe their own press clippings." Others disconnect after they experience significant failure and begin to doubt themselves and God. The result is the same—a loss of true spiritual power and authority.

Those who disconnect go in one of four directions.

- Some have focused on trying to change their lives through rules and external behavioral changes. This is a new form of legalism. It is formula Christianity that is characterized by the notion "If I do this, God does that." Unfortunately, many Christians are giving and serving because they "have to," not because they "want to," and are getting very tired doing it. What they don't realize is that Scripture tells us clearly that if we give or serve with the wrong motives, it is not even considered as giving or serving. C. S. Lewis wrote,

> Our faith is not a matter of our hearing what Christ said long ago and "trying to carry it out." . . . The real Son of God is at your side. He is beginning to turn you into the same kind of thing as Himself. He is beginning, so to speak, to "inject" His kind of life and thought, His Zoe (life), into you; beginning to turn the tin soldier into a live man. The part of you that does not like it is the part that is still tin.[6]

- Some have focused on finding significant "experiences." The problem is that experiences are like some medications; the more you take, the less effect they have. The "highs" get further and further apart, and the "lows" increase in severity.
- Some have given up and decided to just focus on heaven, where things will be different. They assume that virtually all of God's promises are intended only for heaven. Until we are in heaven, we just have to suffer and survive, the thinking goes.
- Some have given up and dropped out; Christianity is hardly a thought. Where their Christian faith used to be vibrant, it has now become irrelevant.

Satan's Plan to Defeat Christian Leaders

Pastors and ministry leaders must recognize that they face a significant enemy who does not want them to succeed. While many Christians do not believe it or act like it is true, Satan has limits in terms of what he is allowed to do. We see in the book of Job how God only let Satan do certain things; he did not have unlimited access to Job.

A principle that comes out clearly in the New Testament is that when we give the enemy some kind of a door, some kind of open opportunity, he is free to come in and harass us. Conflict in the church is one of those doors. Once we give him access, we find it is difficult to remove him. This is true for the individual as well as the church. We are much smarter to keep those doors of access closed rather than try to fight him after he has entered.

Even though the power of Satan is limited, he still has plenty of tactics to try and bring down Christian leaders. What are his common strategies? Let's look at Moses as an example of how Satan tries to defeat God's chosen servants.

The Example of Moses

Moses's life is a study of contrasts. We know that through a set of providential circumstances, Moses was raised in the house of Pharoah. As a result, he received the finest education of his time. However, Moses also knew that he was an Israelite and that there was a call upon his life to lead his people. He was willing to give up the life of the palace to try and help his people. However, his initial attempt was rejected, and because he had killed an Egyptian who was abusing a fellow Hebrew, he fled for his life into the desert. He lived there for approximately forty years.

Moses was a man very much loved by God. In the Scriptures he is referred to as a prophet of God, a man of God, a friend of God, and a servant of God: "And the LORD said to Moses, 'I will do the very thing you have asked, because I am pleased with you and I know you by name'" (Exod. 33:17). Some translations say, "you have found favor with me and you are my friend." This shows God's pleasure with the heart of Moses. In fact, at the end of Deuteronomy the summation of the ministry of Moses reads, "Since then, no prophet has risen in Israel like Moses, whom the LORD knew face to face, who did all those miraculous signs and wonders the LORD sent him to do in Egypt—to Pharaoh and to all his officials and to his whole land. For no one has ever shown the mighty power or performed the awesome deeds that Moses did in the sight of all Israel" (Deut. 34:10–12).

But Moses was not immune from the attacks of Satan to try to weaken and destroy him as a leader. It reminds us of the words in 1 Peter 5:8–9: "Be self-controlled and alert. Your enemy the devil prowls around like a roaring lion looking for someone to devour. Resist him, standing firm in the faith, because you know that your brothers throughout the world are undergoing the same kind of sufferings." What were the tactics Satan used to undermine Moses?

DOUBT

After Moses had been in the desert for forty years, God appeared to him in the burning bush and called him to lead the people of Israel out of Egypt, saying, "And now the cry of the Israelites has reached me, and I have seen the way the Egyptians are oppressing them. So now, go. I am sending you to Pharaoh to bring my people the Israelites out of Egypt" (Exod. 3:9–10).

However, Moses resisted God and responded with five separate questions or concerns. God was not pleased with Moses's resistance to his call and finally declared that Moses's brother Aaron would be the major spokesman instead of Moses: "Then the LORD's anger burned against Moses and he said, 'What about your brother, Aaron the Levite? I know he can speak well. He is already on his way to meet you, and his heart will be glad when he sees you. You shall speak to him and put words in his mouth; I will help both of you speak and will teach you what to do. He will speak to the people for you, and it will be as if he were your mouth and as if you were God to him'" (Exod. 4:14–16).

Moses obeyed, went back to Egypt, and confronted Pharoah, along with his brother Aaron. Pharoah's response was harsh, and he increased the demands upon the Israelite slaves. As a result, the people of Israel began to complain to Moses and Aaron, saying, "May the LORD look upon you and judge you! You have made us a stench to Pharaoh and his officials and have put a sword in their hand to kill us" (Exod. 5:20–21).

Moses immediately questioned God rather than depending on his provision: "O Lord, why have you brought trouble upon this people? Is this why you sent me? Ever since I went to Pharaoh to speak in your name, he has brought trouble upon this people, and you have not rescued your people at all" (Exod. 5:22–23).

God promised Moses that he would free the Israelites from the oppressive slavery of the Egyptians and take them to their own land. Moses went back to his people and told them what God had said, but they would not listen because of their fears. Again, Moses questioned God: "If the Israelites will not listen to me, why would Pharaoh listen to me, since I speak with faltering lips?" (Exod. 6:12).

The first tactic Satan used on Moses was to get him to doubt the real authority and power of God and instead to focus on his circumstances and limited abilities. This reminds us of the warning in James 1:5–8, "If any of you lacks wisdom, he should ask God, who gives generously to all without finding fault, and it will be given to him. But when he asks, he must believe and not doubt, because he who doubts is like a wave of the sea, blown and tossed by the wind. That man should not think he will receive anything from the Lord; he is a double-minded man, unstable in all he does."

DISTRACTION

Distraction causes us to lose focus and to spend our time and energies in the wrong places. There is a principle that states that 20 percent of our efforts will produce 80 percent of the results. That means we must carefully consider how we spend our time. If we major on the minors, we will quickly lose perspective and lose sight of our mission and vision. Some people have called this the "tyranny of the urgent."

Now, obviously we cannot remove every distraction from our lives, nor can we prevent interruptions from occurring. However, we must constantly monitor ourselves to make sure we are not drifting off course. How many pastors or ministry leaders monitor their schedules regularly to make sure that their priorities and values are reflected in their use of time. You can guarantee that if you don't manage your time well, others will manage it for you. And it is unlikely that others will have the focus and perspective God wants for your life.

Another source of distraction is dealing with negative people. We have already seen how these people can cause division, but they also can be a source of distraction. One of the common phenomena in counseling is that people seldom share their real problems or concerns initially. Instead, they share issues and concerns that are peripheral to the real problem. Thus, counselors are trained to ignore what are called the "presenting problems." Instead, they either wait until the individual finally gets to the real problem or use probing questions to get to the real issues.

Many leaders, because they have not been trained in counseling techniques, do not understand what is going on and focus on the wrong problems and issues. By focusing on the wrong issues, even if they are addressed properly, there is no closure or solution to the concerns. This can be a major source of distraction.

A third source of distraction is fatigue. Vince Lombardi, the famous football coach of the Green Bay Packers, said it well: "Fatigue makes cowards of us all." Fatigue causes us to lose sight of our objectives, to lose focus on our ultimate goal. Intentions are not enough to keep us going when the going gets tough. One pastor friend put it this way: "Christ asked me to live for him, not die for him." Many leaders, operating out of a sense of guilt or fear, simply wear themselves out trying to meet all of the expectations of ministry. The result is incredible fatigue that often leads to discouragement and failure.

When we are tired, we revert to old patterns and thoughts, many of which are unproductive. Our perspective is not clear because of the fatigue, and as a result we are easily distracted.

The next attempt of Satan to destroy Moses's leadership of the people of Israel was to try and distract him and get him to focus on the wrong things.

When Moses's father-in-law, Jethro, visited Moses in the desert, he saw that Moses was trying to solve all the people's problems and concerns himself. Moses did not understand the value of delegation.

> Moses' father-in-law replied, "What you are doing is not good. You and these people who come to you will only wear yourselves out. The work is too heavy for you; you cannot handle it alone. Listen now to me and I will give you some advice, and may God be with you. You must be the people's representative before God and bring their disputes to him. Teach them the decrees and laws, and show them the way to live and the duties they are to perform. But select capable men from all the people—men who fear God, trustworthy men who hate dishonest gain—and appoint them as officials over thousands, hundreds, fifties and tens. Have them serve as judges for the people at all times, but have them bring every difficult case to you; the simple cases they can decide themselves. That will make your load lighter, because they will share it with you. If you do this and God so commands, you will be able to stand the strain, and all these people will go home satisfied."
>
> Exodus 18:17–23

It's particularly interesting that God used a non-Israelite to instruct Moses on how he should lead. Moses followed his father-in-law's advice and as a result was freed to do the essential elements of leadership—spending time with God and leading the people of Israel. God then gave Moses the Ten Commandments, the Law, and the instructions on how to build the tabernacle.

DISCOURAGEMENT

Discouragement comes in many forms, but leaders appear to be particularly victimized by this emotion. Think of the numerous examples in Scripture of God's faithful becoming discouraged and losing focus and perspective. Elijah comes immediately to mind (see 1 Kings 19). Whether Elijah was suffering from depression or simple fatigue, it is obvious that Satan was using fear to cause Elijah to lose sight of his mission and vision. Paul, the mighty apostle, also suffered at times from discouragement (see 2 Tim. 4:9–18).

Bill Hybels wrote an incredible article several years ago, titled "Reading Your Emotional Gauges." The thesis of his article was that leaders in particular must constantly monitor their emotional gauges. Hybels indicated that he had done a good job of monitoring his spiritual and physical gauges (his personal devotional life and his physical exercise routine) but had ignored his emotional gauge. He discovered that he was spending too much time around people who were draining him emotionally and not enough time around those who encouraged him emotionally. He likened the draining effect to a battery. A battery needs recharging every now and then, otherwise it becomes useless. Hybels concluded the same was true for leaders.

One of the natural phenomena of leadership is that people with concerns or problems will share them with you. Because most Christians do not understand the basic principles of confronting one another, these people often are judgmental, overly critical of leaders, and filled with anger. There will be a lot more of these kinds of people who will approach leaders than those who come to encourage them. Thus, if the leader simply takes in all of the negative input without carefully evaluating it, he or she may become easily discouraged.

Also, if leaders do not plan their schedule with their emotions in mind, they will not take the time to include activities that provide the necessary encouragement. Each leader is different, but most know the activities or people that encourage them and give them positive energy. Good leaders make sure they balance their schedule to include these positive emotional experiences. Thus, when the negative experiences do come, they are better prepared to "stand firm," as Paul admonished the Corinthians: "Therefore, my dear brothers, stand firm. Let nothing move you. Always give yourselves fully to the work of the Lord, because you know that your labor in the Lord is not in vain" (1 Cor. 15:58).

Satan tried to use discouragement to defeat Moses. As Moses began to lead the people in the desert, they quickly turned against him when things got rough. They constantly were complaining to Moses and questioning God as well, even though God provided miraculously for all their needs.

Unfortunately, this constant complaining wore Moses out, as you can see in his response to God:

> Moses heard the people of every family wailing, each at the entrance to his tent. The LORD became exceedingly angry, and Moses was troubled. He asked the LORD, "Why have you brought this trouble on your servant? What have I done to displease you that you put the burden of all these people on me? Did I conceive all these people? Did I give them birth? Why do you tell me to carry them in my arms, as a nurse carries an infant, to the land you promised on oath to their forefathers? Where can I get meat for all these people? They

keep wailing to me, 'Give us meat to eat!' I cannot carry all these
people by myself; the burden is too heavy for me. If this is how you
are going to treat me, put me to death right now—if I have found
favor in your eyes—and do not let me face my own ruin."

Numbers 11:10–14

Moses gets so discouraged that he asks God to kill him. We see
this response from other leaders in the Bible also. However, this is
not the response God wants. He wants his Christian leaders to trust
him and know that he will provide for their needs. Leading people is
a difficult task, as people will not always appreciate or recognize all
that the leader does for them. If leaders allow complaints to distract
and discourage them, they lose focus and are not able to provide the
leadership they should.

DIVISION

For some reason many Christian leaders are not prepared for conflict
and division, particularly from those closest to them. And yet one of
the most common strategies of Satan is to cause division, particularly
among leaders.

Satan knows that opposition from outside the church normally
strengthens it, so he seldom uses that strategy. Similarly, he seldom
uses people outside the leadership core of the church to initiate conflict, the reason being that they usually do not have the credibility to
do much damage. Therefore, his consistent strategy is to use people
within the leadership circle. But how can he do that? How can he get
godly men and women off track so that they are used for his purpose
of dividing the church?

The answer is simple. He starts with a legitimate grievance. As a
natural course of church life, we all make mistakes and treat one another in hurtful or harmful ways. If we deal with these issues correctly,
extending forgiveness and confronting where necessary, the matter is
ended and Satan gains no foothold.

However, when we fail to deal with these legitimate grievances, they
can become a major source of bitterness and division. We begin to view
other events and actions through a new lens—one that is tainted by
our grievances. We begin to see patterns that don't exist; we begin to
draw conclusions that are invalid. Over time what were very minor
differences can turn into major conflicts.

When this happens among ministry leaders, it has all the potential for devastating consequences. People begin to take sides based on whom they love, trust, or respect. If this is not understood, leaders can get lost in endless struggles.

Moses had to face the rebellion of the two people closest to him, his own brother and sister, Aaron and Miriam. This is the most difficult kind of leadership crisis, when fellow leaders turn against you. Moses once again responds with the ultimate shepherd's heart and asks God to heal Miriam's leprosy. In fact, the Scripture declares, "(Now Moses was a very humble man, more humble than anyone else on the face of the earth.) . . . 'Listen to my words: "When a prophet of the LORD is among you, I reveal myself to him in visions, I speak to him in dreams. But this is not true of my servant Moses; he is faithful in all my house. With him I speak face to face, clearly and not in riddles; he sees the form of the LORD. Why then were you not afraid to speak against my servant Moses?"'" (Num. 12:3, 6–8). From this passage we can see the love God had for Moses as well as Moses's true humility. Moses demonstrated the necessary character qualities to be a great leader and totally defeated the plan of the enemy.

DISILLUSIONMENT

Satan's final strategy was to get Moses so disillusioned in his role as leader that he would become angry and disobey God. Disillusionment occurs when someone is under what seems like a constant barrage of attacks from the enemy. Satan's strategy is gradually to wear down the leader.

Moses had faced constant grumbling from the people of Israel and in most cases held up well, but the challenges to his leadership were not over. In fact, when faced with the opportunity to go into the Promised Land, the people refused to go and supported the ten spies who warned them of the dangers they would face. God responded by saying that he would wipe out the people and make a new nation from the ones who were faithful. Moses again interceded on behalf of the people, and God promised him that although the people who had rebelled would not be allowed to enter the new land, their children would.

Moses faced another rebellion by approximately 250 leaders, including Korah. This time Moses not only interceded for the people of Israel but stood strong against those who had rebelled. He declared that God would destroy them, which he did.

Moses had one more test that, unfortunately, he failed. This was when the people again complained when they did not have enough water at Meribah. When Moses and Aaron sought God, he told them what they were to do: "Take the staff, and you and your brother Aaron gather the assembly together. Speak to that rock before their eyes and it will pour out its water. You will bring water out of the rock for the community so they and their livestock can drink" (Num. 20:8).

Evidently Moses was so angry and frustrated with the people of Israel that instead of speaking to the rock, he struck it with his rod. God's response was severe.

> But the LORD said to Moses and Aaron, "Because you did not trust in me enough to honor me as holy in the sight of the Israelites, you will not bring this community into the land I give them."
>
> Numbers 20:12

> By the waters of Meribah they angered the LORD, and trouble came to Moses because of them; for they rebelled against the Spirit of God, and rash words came from Moses' lips.
>
> Psalm 107:32–33

It appears that Moses still did not understand what was really going on if we read his comments in the book of Deuteronomy: "But because of you the LORD was angry with me and would not listen to me" (Deut. 3:26). Moses seems to be blaming the people for his not being allowed to enter the Promised Land. However, it was because of his own failure to obey God's specific instructions that he was forbidden to cross the Jordan with his people. In Deuteronomy 32:49–52 God states the reason for Moses's severe discipline: "Go up into the Abarim Range to Mount Nebo in Moab, across from Jericho, and view Canaan, the land I am giving the Israelites as their own possession. There on the mountain that you have climbed you will die and be gathered to your people, just as your brother Aaron died on Mount Hor and was gathered to his people. This is because both of you broke faith with me in the presence of the Israelites at the waters of Meribah Kadesh in the Desert of Zin and because you did not uphold my holiness among the Israelites. Therefore, you will see the land only from a distance; you will not enter the land I am giving to the people of Israel."

What a sad and unfortunate conclusion to Moses's career. After all that Moses had gone through, he was not allowed to see the fruit of his efforts because of his own disobedience. However, we must remember that Moses was a very reluctant leader all along the way. Although he had the necessary character qualities to be an outstanding leader, he constantly failed in properly taking up the leadership mantle. He was an outstanding servant but not an outstanding leader. Obviously God was trying to provide everything necessary for Moses to be a successful leader, but Moses failed to see or understand what God was doing and ultimately failed.

Christian leaders must be aware of these strategies of Satan. The first step in defeating these strategies is to recognize what they are. While a gift of discernment would help greatly in this process, every Christian leader can learn to spot Satan's plans and thereby defeat them.

What leaders need is the courage and conviction that Shadrach, Meschach, and Abednego displayed in Daniel 3:16–18. They said, "O Nebuchadnezzar, we do not need to defend ourselves before you in this matter. If we are thrown into the blazing furnace, the God we serve is able to save us from it, and he will rescue us from your hand, O king. But even if he does not, we want you to know, O king, that we will not serve your gods or worship the image of gold you have set up."

James gives a similar warning in James 4:7: "Submit yourselves, then, to God. Resist the devil, and he will flee from you."

The Example of Saul

King Saul is an example of a man chosen by God who failed in both his character development as well as in his leadership ability. Saul had everything going for him as a potential leader.

- He was selected by God to be king of Israel (1 Sam. 10:1).
- Samuel the prophet and judge was his friend and mentor.
- Saul had a naturally imposing stature—"the most handsome man in Israel—head and shoulders taller than anyone else in the land" (1 Sam. 9:2).
- Saul was personally touched by God and empowered to prophesy by the Holy Spirit—"As Saul turned and started to leave, God changed his heart, and all Samuel's signs were fulfilled that day. . . . Then the Spirit of God came upon Saul, and he, too, began to prophesy. When his friends heard about it, they exclaimed, 'What? Is Saul a prophet?'" (1 Sam. 10:9–11).
- Saul had a loyal band of men who followed him and supported him—"When Saul returned to his home at Gibeah, a band of men

whose hearts God had touched became his constant companions"
(1 Sam. 10:26).

Despite all these tremendous advantages, Saul totally failed as a leader.
The first evidence of this came immediately after he was anointed by
the prophet Samuel. When Samuel called a meeting of all of the people
of Israel at Mizpah to present Saul as king, Saul was found hiding in the
baggage. Evidently he was a very reluctant leader from the beginning.

After becoming king, Saul was immediately victorious in a major
battle against the Ammonites. However, his next leadership failure
occurred shortly after this great victory. Samuel had instructed Saul
to wait for him at Gilgal for seven days, where Samuel would then present an offering to God before Saul and his troops went to war against
the Philistines. However, when Samuel didn't arrive as scheduled,
and some of Saul's men began to desert him because of their fear of
the Philistines, Saul went ahead on his own and offered the sacrifice
himself. God's discipline for this leadership failure was severe: "How
foolish!" Samuel exclaimed. "You have disobeyed the command of the
LORD your God. Had you obeyed, the LORD would have established your
kingdom over Israel forever. But now your dynasty must end, for the
LORD has sought out a man after his own heart. The LORD has already
chosen him to be king over his people, for you have not obeyed the
LORD's command" (1 Sam. 13:13–14 NLT).

You would think after this severe rebuke of the Lord that Saul would
understand the importance of following God's instructions exactly.
However, very soon after Samuel told Saul that God wanted him to
attack and totally destroy the Amalekites: "Now go and completely
destroy the entire Amalekite nation—men, women, children, babies,
cattle, sheep, camels, and donkeys" (1 Sam. 15:3 NLT).

After defeating the Amalekites, Saul spared the life of the Amalekite
king and kept the best of the sheep and the cattle. Scripture makes
Saul's motive clear: "Saul and his men spared Agag's life and kept the
best of the sheep and cattle, the fat calves and lambs—everything, in
fact, that appealed to them. They destroyed only what was worthless
or of poor quality" (1 Sam. 15:9 NLT). God spoke clearly to Samuel
about Saul's failure: "Then the LORD said to Samuel, 'I am sorry that
I ever made Saul king, for he has not been loyal to me and has again
refused to obey me.' Samuel was so deeply moved when he heard this
that he cried out to the LORD all that night" (1 Sam. 15:10–11 NLT).

To make the situation even worse, when Samuel confronted Saul,
he lied about the reasons for his disobedience: "'It's true that the army

spared the best of the sheep and cattle,' Saul admitted. 'But they are going to sacrifice them to the LORD your God. We have destroyed everything else'" (1 Sam. 15:15 NLT). Samuel sharply rebuked Saul, saying, "Although you may think little of yourself, are you not the leader of the tribes of Israel? The LORD has anointed you King of Israel. . . . Rebellion is as bad as the sin of witchcraft, and stubbornness is as bad as worshiping idols. So because you have rejected the word of the LORD, he has rejected you from being king" (1 Sam. 15:17, 23 NLT).

Saul did repent finally and admitted that he disobeyed Samuel's instructions and the Lord's command: "For I was afraid of the people and did what they demanded" (1 Sam. 15:24 NLT). Again we see Saul's rejection of his leadership role and responsibilities because of fear. Although he remained the official king of Israel for many years after, he was never the leader he was supposed to be or could have been.

This is a good warning for Christian leaders today. We must be careful to listen to God and follow his instructions regardless of the people around us. We must be both servants *and* leaders. And we must be careful not to allow doubt, distraction, discouragement, division, and disillusionment to keep us from performing our leadership responsibilities.

Summary

Leadership is difficult, sometimes incredibly difficult, but it is not impossible. Learning to move effectively from strategy to tactics is one essential for Christian leaders. Having our well-crafted plans not turn out as we expected is probably more the norm than the exception. Therefore, effective leaders will use their leadership skills to make the necessary adjustments and corrections as they go.

Another key to effective leadership is learning how and why Christian leaders fail and making sure that we don't fall for the same schemes and traps others have before us. It often has surprised me (and a lot of other people when they read the Bible) to discover all of the failures detailed throughout both the Old and New Testament. The reality that is portrayed is a strong confirmation of the accuracy and reliability of the Scriptures. But those failures are there for another major reason, and that is so we can learn and profit from them. What is sad is when we see Christian leaders succumb to destructive patterns in their own lives. On the other hand, it is a great joy when we see Christian leaders take the lessons from Scripture and stand strong throughout their lives.

It is a wonderful testimony to the power and reality of Jesus Christ and what he wants to do for all of us.

Questions for Reflection

1. Do you feel you are personally stronger in the strategic aspects of leadership or the tactical aspects of leadership? What are the implications for your future leadership behavior?
2. In this chapter we identified several tactics used against Moses as he tried to lead the people of Israel. Which of these causes you the most personal difficulty in your leadership capacity? How can you deal with it differently in the future so that it does not negatively impact your ministry?

CONCLUSION

We started by identifying the desperate need today for more Christian leaders. Now we can look back and see why that need is so great as well as how it can be filled. We know that God is doing his part to train and equip the necessary leaders. We must recognize what he is doing and do our part. Churches can greatly improve their training process for emerging leaders, as can the training institutions. Potential leaders can learn the lessons of Scripture regarding leadership and character, thereby shortening the training process. But all of this will require intentional effort on the part of leaders, churches, and training institutions. This intentionality is one of the foundational characteristics of good Christian leadership. Effective leadership development does not happen by accident in our own lives or in the lives of others.

Times may be difficult and Christian leadership may be as difficult as ever, but God's plan has not changed. He has promised to provide both the way and the means to train and equip godly leaders for his church. The apostle Paul said it well: "Not that I have already obtained all this, or have already been made perfect, but I press on to take hold of that for which Christ Jesus took hold of me. Brothers, I do not consider myself yet to have taken hold of it. But one thing I do: Forgetting what is behind and straining toward what is ahead, I press on toward the goal to win the prize for which God has called me heavenward in Christ Jesus" (Phil. 3:12–14). At the end of his life he looked back and made the following assessment of his life: "I have fought the good fight, I have finished the race, I have kept the faith" (2 Tim. 4:7).

All of us who are Christian leaders aim first and foremost at pleasing our Lord and Savior, Jesus Christ. We want to make sure our lives have made a difference, that we have had some impact on the people around us. We desire to fulfill every assignment where God has given us an opportunity to minister, and we want to do so with excellence. In other words, we want our lives to count. We recognize the incredible love God has for us as well as all the things he has entrusted to us. We want to be faithful servants who bring him a significant return on everything he has given us. At the end of our lives we desire to hear the famous words found in several Gospels: "Well done, good and faithful servant! You have been faithful with a few things; I will put you in charge of many things. Come and share your master's happiness!" (Matt. 25:21).

NOTES

Introduction

1. Tony Evans, quoted in Jerry C. Wofford, *Transforming Christian Leadership* (Grand Rapids: Baker, 1999), 9.

2. John Maxwell, *Developing the Leader within You* (Nasville: Thomas Nelson, 1993), 1.

3. Robert K. Greenleaf, *The Power of Servant Leadership* (San Francisco: Berrett-Koehler, 1998), 80.

4. Throughout this book I will refer to people I've met and worked with as a consultant. The names I'll use for these people are fictitious to protect their privacy, but the stories I'll tell are true stories with which I'm familiar on a personal level.

Chapter 1: Leadership Issues in Our Churches Today

1. Aubrey Malphurs, *Maximize Your Effectiveness* (Grand Rapids: Baker, 1995), 11.

2. John Trent, *LifeMapping* (Colorado Springs: Focus on the Family, 1994), 153.

3. Greenleaf, *The Power of Servant Leadership*, 32.

4. Bob Buford, *Game Plan* (Grand Rapids: Zondervan, 1997), 19.

5. George Barna, *The Second Coming of the Church* (Nashville: Word, 1998), 36.

6. Todd Hunter, "Successful Pastors: Are They Really Different?" *Equipping the Saints* (spring 1988): 18.

7. There are several instruments that assess leadership behavior. Blanchard Training and Development, Inc., Calif., in Escondido, sells one version for measuring self (LBAI) and one version for measuring others (LBAII). There are also several manuals that can be purchased that provide additional analysis and information on the concepts covered in the instruments themselves.

8. Blanchard Training and Development, Inc., *Leadership Behavior Analysis*, 1991.

9. Drea Zigarmi, Carl Edeburn, and Kenneth Blanchard, *Getting to Know the LBAII* (Escondido, CA: The Ken Blanchard Companies, 1990), 6.

10. Ibid., 70.

11. Robert Schuller, *Your Church Has Real Possibilities* (Glendale, CA: Gospel Light, 1974), 49.

12. C. Peter Wagner, *Your Church Can Grow* (Glendale, CA: Gospel Light, 1976), 57.

13. C. B. Hogue, *I Want My Church to Grow* (Nashville: Broadman, 1977), 67.

14. Lawrence Richards, *A New Face for the Church* (Grand Rapids: Zondervan, 1970), 130–31.

15. Joe Ellis, *The Church on Purpose* (Cincinnati: Standard, 1982), 131.

16. Richards, *A New Face for the Church*, 227.

17. Paul Hersey and Kenneth Blanchard, *Management of Organizational Behavior* (Englewood Cliffs, NJ: Prentice-Hall, 1977), 71–72.

18. Ted Engstrom, *The Making of a Christian Leader* (Grand Rapids: Zondervan, 1976), 79.

19. Jack Balswick and Walter Wright, "A Complementary-Empowering Model of Ministerial Leadership," *Pastoral Psychology* 37 (fall 1988).

20. Daniel Goleman, *Primal Leadership* (Boston: Harvard Business School Press, 2002), 64.

21. Mike Regele, *Death of the Church* (Grand Rapids: Zondervan, 1995), 96.

22. Malphurs, *Maximize Your Effectiveness*, 58–59.

23. James C. Dobson, *Parenting Isn't for Cowards* (Waco: Word, 1987), 24.

24. *Performax: Personal Profile System*, a personality-style assessment tool (Minneapolis: Carlson Learning).

25. Philip Schaff, *History of the Christian Church* (Oak Harbor, WA: Logos Research Systems, 1997).

Chapter 2: Why We Lack Effective Christian Leadership

1. Rick Warren, quoted in C. Peter Wagner, *Churchquake* (Ventura, CA: Regal, 1999), 89–90.

2. Grace Murray Hopper, quoted in Pat Riley, *Winner Within* (New York: G. P. Putnam's Sons, 1993), 161.

3. Jerry C. Wofford, *Transforming Christian Leadership* (Grand Rapids: Baker, 1999), 16.

4. Greenleaf, *The Power of Servant Leadership*, 208.

5. Alan Nelson and Stan Toler, *The 5 Secrets to Becoming a Leader* (Ventura, CA: Regal, 2002), 30.

6. Noel M. Tichy and Stratford Sherman, *Control Your Destiny or Someone Else Will* (New York: Doubleday, 1993), 151.

7. Bill Parcells, *Finding a Way to Win* (New York: Doubleday, 1995), 97.

8. Warren Bennis and Burt Nanus, *Leaders* (New York: Harper & Row, 1985), 22.

9. Warren Bennis, *On Becoming a Leader* (Reading, MA: Addison-Wesley, 1989), 45.

10. Harry Truman, quoted in *The Edge* (Cleveland: Getting The Edge, 1991), 2–31.

11. Parcells, *Finding a Way to Win*, 84.

12. Lyle Schaller, quoted in Wagner, *Churchquake*, 74.

13. F. F. Bruce, *The Spreading Flame* (Grand Rapids: Eerdmans, 1958), 189.

14. Ralph Burnett, "Sold on Risk Taking," *World Traveler*, March 1996, 48.

15. Mark Dever, *Nine Marks of a Healthy Church* (Wheaton: Crossway, 2000), 212.

16. James Emery White, *Rethinking the Church* (Grand Rapids: Baker Books, 1997), 100.

17. Wagner, *Your Church Can Grow*, 61.

18. George Barna, *The Index of Leading Spiritual Indicators* (Dallas: Word, 1996), 118.

19. Rick Warren, *The Purpose-Driven Church* (Grand Rapids: Zondervan, 1995), 31.

20. Carl F. George and Robert E. Logan, *Leading and Managing Your Church* (Old Tappan, NJ: Revell, 1987), 148.

21. Barna, *The Second Coming of the Church*, 105.

Chapter 3: Ministry Leadership and Organizational Structure

1. Howard Clark Kee, Franklin W. Young, and Karlfried Froehlich, *Understanding the New Testament* (Englewood Cliffs, NJ: Prentice-Hall, 1973), 146.

2. *The New Bible Dictionary* (Wheaton: Tyndale, 1962).

3. Ibid.

4. Ibid.

Chapter 4: Defining Leadership

1. Maxwell, *Developing the Leader within You*, introduction.

2. Brian Tracy, *Leadership: The Critical Difference* (video series, Brian Tracy International, Solana Beach, CA).

3. Henry Blackaby and Richard Blackaby, *Spiritual Leadership* (Nashville: Broadman & Holman, 2001), 20.

4. J. Oswald Sanders, *Spiritual Leadership* (Chicago: Moody, 1967), 104.

5. George and Logan, *Leading and Managing Your Church*, 41.

6. James M. Kouzes and Barry Z. Posner, *The Leadership Challenge* (San Francisco: Jossey-Bass, 1987), 277.

7. Bernard Montgomery, quoted in John Maxwell, *The 21 Indispensable Qualities of a Leader* (Nashville: Thomas Nelson, 1999), 1.

8. Thomas E. Cronin, quoted in Burt Nanus and Stephen M. Dobbs, *Leaders Who Make a Difference* (New York: John Wiley & Sons, 1999), 7.

9. Max DePree, *Leadership Is an Art* (New York: Dell Publishing, 1989), 1.

10. M. L. Chemers, "Leadership Theory and Research: A Systems-Process Integration," in *Basic Group Processes*, ed. P. B. Paulus (New York: Springer-Verlag, 1983), 28.

11. Alan McMahan, "Training Turn-Around Leaders" (doctoral dissertation, Fuller Theological Seminary, 1998), 84.

12. J. Robert Clinton, *The Making of a Leader* (Colorado Springs: NavPress, 1988), 213.

13. Leighton Ford, *Transforming Leadership* (Downers Grove, IL: InterVarsity, 1991), 15–16.

14. Robert E. Logan, *Beyond Church Growth* (Old Tappan, NJ: Revell, 1989), 40–41.

15. Balswick and Wright, "A Complementary-Empowering Model of Ministerial Leadership," 8.

16. Maxwell, *Developing the Leader within You,* 1.

17. Nelson and Toler, *The 5 Secrets,* 64.

Chapter 5: God's Training Process for Christian Leaders

1. Clinton, *The Making of a Leader,* 13.

2. Sanders, *Spiritual Leadership,* 18.

Chapter 6: God's Growth Processes

1. Helen Keller, quoted in *The Edge,* 1–9.

Chapter 7: The Coaching Model for Christian Leadership

1. Regele, *Death of the Church,* 222.

2. Bill Walsh, *Building a Champion* (New York: St. Martin's Press, 1990), 60–61.

3. Goleman, *Primal Leadership,* 60.

4. Tichy and Sherman, *Control Your Destiny,* 151.

5. Dallas Willard, *The Divine Conspiracy* (San Francisco: HarperCollins, 1998), 15.

6. Bennis, *On Becoming a Leader,* 143.

7. Tichy and Sherman, *Control Your Destiny,* 132.

8. Greenleaf, *The Power of Servant Leadership,* 114.

9. Elmer Towns, *America's Fastest Growing Churches* (Nashville: Impact, 1972), 203.

10. Ellis, *The Church on Purpose,* 131.

11. James M. Kouzes and Barry Z. Posner, *Credibility* (San Francisco: Jossey-Bass, 1993), 16.

12. Nelson and Toler, *The 5 Secrets,* 47.

13. Bennis, *On Becoming a Leader,* 111–12.

14. John Wooden, quoted in *The Edge,* 2–22.

15. Kouzes and Posner, *Credibility,* 16.

16. Warren, *The Purpose-Driven Church,* 42.

17. Jim Dethmer, *Ministry Advantage* 5, no. 6 (July/August 1994): 4.

18. James M. Kouzes and Barry Z. Posner, *The Leadership Challenge* (San Francisco: Jossey-Bass, 1987), 21–22. Also see, by the same authors, *Credibility.*

19. Kouzes and Posner, *Credibility,* 25.

20. Joe Paterno, quoted in *The Edge*, 1–17.

21. Peter Drucker, *Managing the Nonprofit Organization* (New York: HarperCollins, 1990), 151.

22. Parcells, *Finding a Way to Win*, 12.

23. Quoted in *Ministry Advantage* 5, no. 6 (July/Aug. 1994): 3.

24. Theodore Roosevelt, quoted in James C. Collins and Jerry I. Porras, *Built to Last* (New York: HarperCollins, 1994), 91.

25. Walter Cottingham, quoted in *The Edge*, 2–18.

26. Tom Peters, *Seattle Post-Intelligencer*, 2 December 1991, B4.

27. Blanton Collier, quoted in *The Edge*, 5–30.

28. George Hunter, quoted in Brian McLaren, *Reinventing Your Church* (Grand Rapids: Zondervan, 1998), 116.

29. Don Simmons, in Leadership Network, *Explorer*, May 2001.

30. Robert E. Coleman, *The Master Plan of Evangelism* (Old Tappan, NJ: Revell, 1963), 18.

31. Gene Getz, *Sharpening the Focus of the Church* (Chicago: Moody, 1980), 166.

32. Harry Truman, quoted in *The Edge*, 4–14.

33. Martin Seligman, *Learned Optimism* (New York: Alfred A. Knopf, 1991), 4–5.

34. Ibid., 44–50.

35. John Maxwell, *Failing Forward* (Nashville: Thomas Nelson, 2000), 38.

36. Erma Bombeck, quoted in Maxwell, *Failing Forward*, 25.

Chapter 8: Designing a Personal Development Plan

1. Goleman, *Primal Leadership*, 140.

2. Ibid., 96–97, 101.

3. For a much more detailed description of strategic planning in a church environment, see my book *Ministry Playbook: Strategic Planning for Effective Churches* (Grand Rapids: Baker, 2002).

4. Trent, *LifeMapping*, 16.

5. Søren Kierkegaard, quoted in Bob Buford, *Game Plan* (Grand Rapids: Zondervan, 1997), 67.

6. Goleman, *Primal Leadership*, 116.

7. Trent, *Life Mapping*, 17.

8. For more information, call (734) 904-2760 or write to Church Consultants Group, 3416 Huron View Court, Suite B, Dexter, MI 48130.

9. From the Master's Coach Certification, Church Consultants Group, Dexter, MI.

Chapter 9: Dealing with External Issues That Influence Leadership Effectiveness

1. Spencer Johnson, *Who Moved My Cheese?* (New York: G. P. Putnam's Sons, 1998), 16.
2. Goleman, *Primal Leadership*, 195.
3. Greenleaf, *The Power of Servant Leadership*, 87.
4. The items on this list were taken from the Matrix Grid produced by Doug Anderson of Nehemiah Ministries, Burnsville, MN.
5. Gene Getz, *Elders and Leaders* (Chicago: Moody, 2003).
6. Greenleaf, *The Power of Servant Leadership*, 147.

Chapter 10: Leading in Difficult Times

1. J. M. Barrie, quoted in Maxwell, *Failing Forward*, 1.
2. Joe Paterno, quoted in *The Edge*, 7–8.
3. Sanders, *Spiritual Leadership*, 89.
4. Willard, *The Divine Conspiracy*, xv.
5. Ibid., xiv.
6. C. S. Lewis, quoted in Willard, *The Divine Conspiracy*, 20.

Henry Klopp is president of the International Graduate School of Ministry (www.igsmin.com), a training institute for church leaders. He holds a doctor of ministry degree in the field of church growth and has done graduate work at both Fuller Theological Seminary and the California Graduate School of Theology. Klopp speaks at conferences across the county and resides in Bellevue, Washington. He can be reached via email at hklopp@igsmin.com.